PEO 571

FREDERICK LAW OLMSTED
Partner with Nature

FREDERICK LAW OLMSTED
Partner with Nature

Johanna Johnston

Illustrated with photographs and reproductions

DODD, MEAD & COMPANY · NEW YORK

Design for suspended lamp appearing on chapter opening pages is used with permission and through the courtesy of the Museum of the City of New York.

Library of Congress Cataloging in Publication Data

Johnston, Johanna.
  Frederick Law Olmsted.

  Bibliography: p.
  Includes index.
  SUMMARY: A biography of the self-taught landscape architect who designed many large park systems, including the first large city park in America, Central Park in New York.
  1. Olmsted, Frederick Law, 1822–1903—Juvenile literature. 2. Parks—United States—Juvenile literature. 3. Landscape architecture—United States—Juvenile literature. [1. Olmsted, Frederick Law, 1822–1903. 2. Parks. 3. Landscape architects] I. Title.

SB470.O5J63   712′.092′4 [B] [92]   74–25519
ISBN 0–396–07079–5

Copyright © 1975 by Johanna Johnston
All rights reserved
No part of this book may be reproduced in any form
without permission in writing from the publisher
Printed in the United States of America

CONTENTS

What artist, so noble . . . as he who . . . sketches the outline, writes the colors, and directs the shadows of a picture so great that Nature shall be employed upon it for generations . . .

FREDERICK LAW OLMSTED

PROLOGUE

The city rises up all around, tower on tower, a million windowed walls facing a million other windowed walls. There are narrow streets, crammed with cars, trucks, busses. Looking up, people may see a stretch of sky, but looking around they see only concrete, steel, traffic, and hundreds of nameless people hurrying by.

In the center of all this, there is a great, long oasis. Grassy meadows, low hills edged with greenery, winding paths, lakes studded with small islands, long vistas crowned with trees that almost shut out the city looming on every side. There are open malls where people can stroll, wide fields where games can be played. There it is—the park. New York's Central Park. The park that belongs to everybody—poor, rich, old, young, who come from every part of the city to amble down the paths, sit on the grass, row boats on the lake, or ride bicycles. For all of them, it is the one opportunity the city offers to breathe the smell of green, growing things, to see the various shapes of nature, to find comfort in country scenery.

It is not just a happy accident that these acres of land in the center of the city are as they are. It is not just the luck of New York that the shape of the land is so beautiful, that streams meander past picturesque rocks, that trees and shrubs of a hundred different varieties cluster or spread out in endlessly changing views.

There was a time when all these acres were wasteland, knobbing up here and there with some jumbled rocks, sunken here and there into swampy marshes, spotted with a few squatters' shacks, and populated chiefly by wild pigs and random goats.

There was a time when a young man stood on one of the rises on the eastern side of the land and looked out over the dreary scene. He was a slender figure in a caped coat. He had a thoughtful face and eyes that were curiously intent. He looked westward over the empty expanse to where Manhattan Island was bounded by the Hudson River. He looked eastward toward the river on that side. He looked to the south, where half a mile or so away, the city dribbled to its limits with scattered houses and stables.

And all the while he was looking, he was thinking of three things—the land, and what it might become—the people who lived in the city and what their needs were—and finally, perhaps most of all, the future. How many more people might there be in the city in ten, twenty, or forty years? How might the city itself change in that time?

Land—people—the future. Actually, the young man had been concerned one way or another with those things most of his life, but now, at last, they were all coming together. He could hardly believe his luck. He, Frederick Law Olmsted, was going to help in designing and creating America's first park. It seemed almost like magic, for he had come such a long, roundabout way to this moment.

THE LAND
1822-1836

When he was born, April 26, 1822, there was no such thing as a park in the United States, and no need for one. The country was settled only along the eastern seaboard and not very heavily settled even there. Cities were small, towns even smaller. Hartford, Connecticut, where he was born, was the capital of the state, but it was a little place. Its streets were lined with trees. Every house had its lawn, its garden, generally a barn for the family horse and cow. The Olmsted house, at the edge of town, was practically in the country, with fields and woods beyond it.

And so, like most children in those years, young Fred knew the pleasures of the out-of-doors from the beginning of his life. He ran and tumbled in the grass. He climbed trees. When he began to go to the Dame's School, he splashed and dabbled in the stream that ran behind it and built dams to make pools for holding the tadpoles he and the other children caught.

But he also began to have another way of enjoying the out-of-doors at an early age—thanks to his father. John Olmsted was a businessman, the owner of a thriving dry-goods store on Hartford's main street. He dealt in Holland cloth, wool, satin, and toile. He stocked thread, needles, pins, braids, ribbons—all the things the women of Hartford needed to make clothes for themselves and their families. He was a very quiet, practical sort of man. But he had one great hobby. He loved beautiful scenery, grand views, and picturesque landscapes.

Just as some men collect paintings or objects of art, John Olmsted collected scenery. Every summer he planned a trip to some different part of New England, New York, or New Jersey where he thought there might be good viewing. The whole family went along on these journeys, traveling in the family carriage drawn by the family horse. They bounced and jostled over rutted dirt roads. They choked on dust or were mired in mud. They spent the nights in inns that were dirty and uncomfortable. But they saw some magical things.

One summer they traveled down the Connecticut River valley to Long Island Sound. Another year they went up and over the White Mountains of New Hampshire. Still another summer they went westward to the Hudson River and there they boarded one of those exciting new inventions, a steamboat, and churned down the river to view the battlements of the military academy atop the palisades at West Point. On another journey they traveled by canal boat on the new Erie Canal, westward through the lush valleys of New York, all the way to Niagara Falls, surely the most dramatic scenery John Olmsted had yet viewed.

Young Fred had no idea that he was learning anything from these trips, seeing that people could make land more beautiful by using it well, or make it ugly by using it badly. He thought of learning as going to school, and that had been pleasant enough in the beginning. Two years at the Dame's School, learning his ABCs, had been livened by play and laughter. Then when he was six, his father had decided that the boy should be privately educated by a minister. The teacher-minister he found lived on a farm near New Guilford, and took a few boys each year to live in his home.

Fred enjoyed the months he spent with the Reverend Whittaker and his family. When lessons were over, the boys could roam about the farm as they wished, helping the farmer's wife, or the hired men, with whatever work was in progress. Fred became acquainted with all sorts of farm activities. He and the other boys rode along on the wagon that took grain to the mill to be ground, or rode with the apples to the cider press. They watched the hog-butchering in the fall and the sausage making. They helped the farmer's wife make soap and dip candles. Now and then they herded the cows, fed the chickens, and gathered eggs.

Fred never knew why his father did not send him back to the Reverend Whittaker the next fall. In fact, when he grew up and looked back on the years of his schooling, he was baffled by the course it had followed. His father, so competent in the dry-goods business, so sure of what was good and fine in the way of scenery, seemed completely unsure of how Fred should be educated.

Did it have something to do with the fact that Fred's mother had died when he was only four, soon after his younger brother, John, was born? Had young Fred become an overly intense little boy after that, so that his father worried about him? Fred did not remember anything about his mother's death. He had only one memory of her, a picture of a woman sitting on the grass under a tree, sewing, while he played nearby. And that was always a happy memory.

He remembered very little about the year after his mother's

death, when he and his brother were cared for by aunts. Then
his father married again, a precise and pious woman who was
eager to be a good stepmother to the little boys. Within a
year or so, there was a new baby in the family cradle, a half
sister for Fred and John, and as the years passed, more babies
came along, two more sisters and a brother.

Nobody ever recorded that Fred behaved badly through all
of this. But he did wander a great deal. He would disappear
from home in the morning to ramble through the woods and
meadows, to stop in at the home of some aunt or uncle for
lunch, and then drift on again, not coming home until nightfall. Nobody scolded him. His family did not think he would
come to any harm. But he must have showed some restlessness
that bothered his father. John Olmsted began shifting Fred
from school to school until finally he found another minister
who boarded and tutored boys—the Reverend Brace.

The Reverend Brace boarded the boys who were his stu-
dents in a flimsy building next to his own house. On the
ground floor there were a stable and storage room. The boys
slept and had their lessons in a big room on the second floor.
The room was heated by a wood stove and the boys took turns
in splitting logs for the stove in the yard below and then
hauling the wood upstairs to keep the fire going. This exer-
cise did not bother Fred too much. He did not mind sleeping
on the hard pallets provided for him and the other boys. He
could crack the ice in the wash basin to wash each morning.
What really bothered him was the deathly chill that surrounded the Reverend Brace.

Each morning the minister would mount the stairs and
gaze coldly at his charges. Then he would pray for a long
time. Recitation time came next and if a boy hesitated or
made a mistake, the minister froze him with a glance and then
launched into a sermon about the punishment God had pre-

pared for idlers. Not waiting for that to take effect, the minister generally offered some punishment of his own, rapping the boy's knuckles with his ruler, or, for worse offenses, thrashing him.

Fred had never known anything like this and it horrified him. He began to hate learning, to hate any talk of religion, and above all, to hate the Reverend Brace.

At home for the summer vacation, Fred tried to tell his father how unhappy he was with the Reverend Brace. But John Olmsted, generally so sympathetic, somehow could not believe that a minister could be wrong in any way. He had an idea that Fred needed discipline and Fred's complaints only made him more sure of it. He sent Fred back again to the Reverend Brace that fall, and the next year and the next.

Returning home to Hartford in the spring of 1836, when he was fourteen, Fred wondered if there were any way on earth he could avoid going back to the Reverend Brace again in the fall. He could not think of any argument he had not already used.

And then he tangled with the poison sumac. Surely he did not do it on purpose. Surely he knew the woods and meadows around his home well enough to know that certain small sumac trees with velvety red cockades of bloom gave forth a sap that caused a terrible itching rash in humans.

Still, somehow, Fred did get involved with the poison sumac. One evening, at home after a ramble, he began to itch. His stepmother and father saw that his face was inflamed. His neck and arms were also covered with a rash. They hurried for some of the home remedies that everyone used for such emergencies.

But Fred had contracted such a case of poisoning that these remedies did no good. The next day, when Fred's eyes were swollen almost shut, the doctor was called. He prescribed more poultices and medications. Even so, Fred's sufferings continued. The doctor began to worry about possible damage to his eyesight.

After a week or so, some of Fred's rash and blisters began to fade. But the doctor still was grave when he examined Fred's eyes. "No reading for a while," he said. Later he talked with Fred's father and stepmother.

That evening John Olmsted tried to break it gently to Fred. The doctor did not think that his eyes were going to be permanently affected, but to be on the safe side, he had suggested that Fred not go back to school in the fall.

Fred could hardly believe it at first. Nature, in an unkind mood, had worked a miracle for him. He did not have to go back to the Reverend Brace.

THE PEOPLE
1836-1843

It was 1836, and the world was changing—differently and more rapidly than ever before. A flood of new inventions was causing a revolution in the way people worked and lived. There were more and more steamboats on rivers. Here and there, tracks were being laid to prepare the way for that new travel wonder, the steam railway. New machines were being invented to do many kinds of work that had always been done at home in the past. Factories were springing up to house these machines.

Along with all this, the United States was growing, spreading westward, its population increasing. More and more people were coming from Europe, lured by the promise of a better life. Many moved inland to the unsettled lands in the West, but many more remained in the cities. New York grew larger every year.

None of this made much more impression on Fred than it

would on any teen-aged boy. All that mattered to him was that he was free. The doctor had said that sea-bathing might be good for his eyes, so he went to visit family friends who lived on Long Island Sound. He came home to ramble the countryside, sometimes alone, but often with his brother John, who was old enough now to be a good companion.

John went off to school in the fall and Fred was sorry to see him go, but he did not envy him. He was happy to go on rambling. Actually, his eyes were better now. He could do a little reading. On rainy days, he leafed through the books in his father's library. He especially enjoyed several books on English landscapes that had dark, rich illustrations. He went to the Hartford library and found other books on fine scenery and landscapes in England and other countries. Landscaping, it seemed, was a hobby for rich men, who could transform the vast acres of their estates into beautiful private parks. Still, Fred could not see why the land around his own home could not be improved a little. He suggested to his father that they plant some trees along one side of the property to improve the view in that direction. His father agreed. So Fred busied himself locating some trees that were right for transplanting, and then in arranging for their planting and care.

Now and then, when his father had to take a business trip, Fred went along, visiting New York with him, and the straggling new city of Washington, D.C., and the much older, more dignified city of Philadelphia.

For a year and a half this pleasant life continued. And then John Olmsted decided that Fred was well enough to begin studying something. What should it be? he asked Fred. Fred had no idea. John Olmsted cast about for suggestions. Finally it occurred to him that since Fred was so fond of the out-of-doors he might study surveying and engineering. Fred had no objections to this. And so it was decided. John Olmsted heard of a man in Andover, Massachusetts, who took private pupils to study engineering. And in the fall of 1838, Fred was in Andover, a pupil of Mr. Barton.

Mr. Barton was a pleasant man, nothing like the terrible Reverend Brace. Andover was a pleasant town. This made up somewhat for the fact that Fred found surveying and civil engineering rather boring subjects. So many rods or chains ENE of a rock SSW of a lumber road seemed a dull way to describe a beautiful little glen. He worked at his studies, all the same, and learned some of the principles and skills of surveying. He learned to map the contours of land, to sketch buildings and roads in a certain perspective.

He stuck at it, all told, for two years, with various visits home for holidays and vacations. And then, finally, he felt he had had enough.

His father took the news quietly. He was sure that his intense, emotional oldest son had the intelligence and character to achieve a good and useful life. The only question was—in what field?

"So. What would you like to study, Fred?" he asked.

But once again, Fred really had no idea.

And once again, John Olmsted racked his brains. There was no use thinking of any of the professions, like medicine, for which John was preparing, or the law. Fred had lost too much schooling. John Olmsted thought of his own career. Perhaps Fred could follow in his steps and be a merchant. It was worth a try. He asked Fred if he would like to apprentice himself to some dry-goods importing house in New York and see how he liked it.

Once again, Fred could not think of any objections. And so, in August, 1840, John Olmsted and Fred were driving from Hartford to New York. Fred was being introduced as a new clerk for the firm of Benkard and Hutton, on Beaver Street, and then, a good boarding house having been recommended in Brooklyn Heights, he and his father were ferrying across the East River to find the house and get him settled. Before long, Fred was established in a small room under the eaves. The charge was $3.50 a week, including breakfast and laundry. John Olmsted said good-bye, clucked to the horse, and was off, and Fred was starting a new career.

Fred had been in New York before but being there as a visitor was quite different from becoming a part of the city's bustle and excitement each morning when he stepped off the ferry from Brooklyn.

People! So many people! So many different kinds of people! On the wharves he saw sailors from all over the world, carters, wagonmen, all sorts of odd-job men, and then farther on, there were the merchants who handled ships' supplies. Farther on again, he passed the well-dressed businessmen, their pantaloons strapped under their boots, on their way to banks, law offices, the stock exchange. And all along the way there were the vendors of hot corn on the cob, gingerbread, oysters, or apples. There were newsboys calling their different papers. Here and there, he saw ladies, bonneted and gloved, holding their skirts up a little from the dust or mud, as they made their careful way to some shop. Here and there, he saw a black man or woman, intent on some errand, or suddenly stopping to laugh with a friend at some joke. Here and there, he saw an Oriental face.

Fred was entranced. So many different people made for a sort of stimulation that did not exist in a little city like Hartford. So many different people gathered together meant that some were involved in theaters, in putting on concerts, in giving lectures. There was somebody, somewhere, involved in almost anything one could think of.

At the same time, so many people gathered together meant

that there was more poverty than he had ever seen in Hartford. There were people living in hovels or mean rooms, people picking over rags, or begging. There were people to whom all the theaters, the concerts, the shops, the carriages were nothing but a blurred background to their own lives of hunger and illness and grinding labor.

Fred looked at it all and absorbed and learned more than he knew.

Meantime, of course, he had his job with the dry-goods firm and that was a good deal less interesting. Most of the time he sat on a high stool, checking over invoices and bills and entering figures in long columns. He was a conscientious worker and did so well that his pleased employers were soon giving him more responsibilities. Still, Fred found that the best part of his job was being sent now and then to the wharves to check on incoming shipments. The sights and sounds and smells of the waterfront were endlessly entertaining to him. But his work only took him there once a week or so. The rest of his working time was spent on the high stool before the desk with a quill pen and bills of lading.

He stuck it for almost eighteen months, with frequent visits to Hartford to refresh himself. But finally, in the spring of 1842, just about the time he was celebrating his twentieth birthday, he went home to Hartford to tell his father that it really would not do. He was not cut out to be a merchant.

It was about now that John Olmsted began to think of his oldest son as having a "truant disposition." He remembered him as a small boy, wandering away from home in the morning, not to return till nightfall. He remembered him going from teacher to teacher and finally leaving school altogether. Then there had been his brief efforts to become an engineer. Now this. Was Fred going to be a truant all his life?

Fortunately, this time Fred himself had an idea about what

he wanted to do next. He wanted to go to sea.

John Olmsted was not as astonished as he might have been. His own father, Benjamin Olmsted, had taken to a seafaring life after fighting in the Revolution. Two of his uncles had fought at sea against the British and another had gone into the China trade after the war and made a tidy amount of money. Perhaps seafaring was in Fred's blood and this would be the answer to all his indecision.

So he mulled over the idea and finally nodded. They would look into it, he said. Meantime, there was no need to do anything right away. He wanted both Fred and John, who was not strong, to build up their health during the summer. He thought it might be good for them both to learn fencing and to do a lot of sailing on the river.

With such activities, the summer was a cheerful one. Then, come September, it was time for John to ride off to New Haven, forty miles away, to enroll as a freshman at Yale College. A month or so later, Fred traveled down for a visit, to see how his brother was getting on, to get acquainted with his roommate, a young man named Charles Brace, and to talk some more about his plans for going to sea.

The young men talked rather solemnly about the hardships the life might entail. They had all read a new and popular book by Richard Henry Dana, Jr., *Two Years Before the Mast*, describing his adventures in the forecastle. Still, for all the difficulties of life at sea, there was a challenge about it and a sense of high adventure that appealed to them all.

But still there was no hurry about anything. China-bound ships—and one of those was what Fred wanted—did not leave Atlantic ports until the early spring so that they would avoid winter storms in the China Sea.

Finally, by mid-March of 1843, Fred was traveling to New York to see if he could get a berth. This was not such an easy job for a "green boy" who had never been to sea. But with the help of John Olmsted's connections. Fred at last was talking to Captain Fox, of the bark *Ronaldson*, which was to sail in a month or so for Canton. After some hesitation, Captain Fox finally agreed to sign on the young man.

Fred hurried back to Hartford to make his preparations. John came home from Yale to spend the last week with him. Little sisters, aunts, uncles, and of course, his father and step-mother clustered about, offering advice, as Fred collected shirts, pants, oilskin suit and hat, an almanac, and a quadrant to pack in his little sea chest. At the last moment, Aunt Maria hurried up with a remedy for seasickness and made sure he tucked that in the chest as well.

Finally he was waving good-bye to the family, all but his father and brother who were driving him to New York. Then, just a few days later, he was walking up the gangplank of the *Ronaldson*, lugging his chest. He stood at the rail, waving to his father and brother whom he would not see for a year. But the mate was already calling out orders. The sails were shuddering up the mast. Fred realized someone was shouting an order at him. He took one last look at his father and brother and hurried to see what was wanted of him.

Soon the anchor was raised, a breeze filled the sails, and the *Ronaldson* was moving slowly from her berth, out onto the river, and then toward the Narrows and finally the open ocean.

It was just a week before his twenty-first birthday when Fred began his life at sea.

AT SEA
1843-1844

The ship plunged downward into the trough of a wave, lurched upward, plunged downward again, and Fred lay in a small forecastle bunk, unable to eat, drink, or care if he lived or died. He had talked cheerfully about seasickness when he was on shore, but he had never dreamed it would be like this. And who could have guessed that the *Ronaldson* would run into one squall after another as soon as she was out on the Atlantic?

Aunt Maria's seasick remedy was in his sea chest which had been buried deep under a pile of ship's gear soon after he came aboard. He had forgotten it anyway. Fortunately, one young shipmate was sympathetic and brought him gruel, which he could not eat. Also the ship carried two passengers, one of whom was a doctor, and he looked in on Fred now and then. But nothing really helped.

Finally, after ten days of suffering, Fred was able to get on his feet. Thin, pale, and trembling, he made his way to the deck. At once he was set to the endless drudgery that was the lot of a "green boy." Hour after hour, he scraped rust from anchors and other ironwork. Hour after hour, he emptied buckets that caught the flow from the bilge pump. He stood his watches, four off and four on, and was so exhausted that he fell asleep standing up. Afraid of being washed overboard in such a state, he rigged up various traps to rouse him when he dozed off. He could gain no strength from food. By the time the *Ronaldson* was a month out of New York, all her fresh stores were gone. Meals consisted of half-spoiled meat, moldy beans, and hardtack. And the weather continued bad.

Worse than any of this, however, was the general mood of the ship, which was set by her captain. On every ship, in those years, the captain was absolute master and when the captain was an intelligent, civilized man, a crew could find its life not so hard. But Captain Fox, smooth-talking on shore, became a tyrant on board. He stamped about, pleased with nothing, falling into rages, and cursing everyone. True, most of the crew members were rough, ignorant men recruited from waterfront bars when they were too drunk to know what they were doing. But Fred could not help thinking that a more reasonable form of discipline would have encouraged even these unattractive characters to work more effectively. Instead, the ship simmered with the anger, the discontent, the resentment of the men, while the captain shouted and raged at every one.

And, of course, there was no escape from any of this as the voyage went on, day after day after day. The route to China, in those years, was the long southern swoop through the South Atlantic, around the tip of South America through the terrifying straits of Cape Horn, and then on westward through the Southern Pacific, and at last, past New Guinea into the Java Sea.

They were almost three months out of New York when they anchored off Java Head, to take on water and fresh food. Here Fred and the other men could leave letters for home to be carried by the next New York-bound ship. And then they were off again, making for the China Sea.

Hong Kong, the island off the southern coast of China which was the deep-sea port for Canton, was to have been their next stop. But when they came into Hong Kong harbor they learned from men on other ships anchored there that a terrible plague was raging ashore and it was unsafe for anyone to land.

So Captain Fox sailed the *Ronaldson* out again, and then up the Pearl River toward Canton, eighty miles upriver from the sea.

Canton—fabled name, conjuring up all the hidden mystery of the Orient. Canton—only recently reopened to western traders after the Opium War, and the one city where Fred could hope to glimpse something of China. However, Captain Fox decided to anchor the *Ronaldson* several miles from the ancient city, between sandflats and islands, among a throng of other ships, some familiar-looking western vessels from England and the United States, but most of them local sampans and junks.

Now days went by with no members of the crew allowed to leave the ship and go ashore. Instead, merchants from the hongs, or warehouses, came out to the ship in their sampans to trade with Captain Fox aboard the *Ronaldson*. Fred had an opportunity to notice the politeness of these Chinese traders and their fondness for drinking tea. He was also interested in the way they dressed in long robes, and the way they braided their hair into long queues, of which they were very proud.

At last Captain Fox decided to visit Canton in a small boat.

Fred volunteered to help with the oars and so was able to go along. Bending to his oar as they made their way upstream, Fred finally saw slanting reddish roofs showing above the city walls. The roofs were spiked here and there by red flag poles, and towering over the whole scene were two wonderfully intricate pagodas.

Fred gazed and marveled. He had been looking at views all his life. What did he make of this view, so foreign to all the landscapes or cityscapes that he had ever known? He did not say much about it in his letters home. Instead, he wrote of calling on the American medical missionary in the city to whom he had a letter of introduction. He wrote of some street sights, and the way the people looked—little boys dressed in long, rich robes, exactly like their fathers', women with their hair fantastically dressed, and hobbling on bound feet.

Back on the ship, still moored at its anchorage, Fred soon became sick again. Half the men on board were ill. Perhaps they had some tropical fever. Perhaps they were simply exhausted by their poor diet and miserable lives. No one seemed to know, but there were mutterings among the men about the captain's failure to lay in stores of fresh food for the crew although he was taking proper care to get some good things for himself. Fred just lay on his bunk, lightheaded with fever, dreaming of the comforts of home which he had always taken so much for granted before.

When he recovered from this bout of fever, he was even thinner than he had been. Still, he made visits ashore to the little town near which they were moored. He and a few shipmates wandered about, gazing at shops and houses, gardens and cemeteries. Once more, Fred was aware of the politeness of the Chinese. But nothing he saw seemed to touch him closely. It was all remote and strange.

The *Ronaldson's* cargo of ginseng roots and notions from

the States was finally traded and unloaded. The ship was re-loaded with the return cargo of tea and silk. After many de-lays, orders were given to get under way.

It hardly seemed possible that the return voyage could have been worse than the one going out. But it was. Most of the food aboard was spoiled. The weather was frequently bad. And the captain's temper was so vicious, the punishments he meted out so ferocious, that the crew actually began to talk about mutiny.

One old sailor argued restraint. He warned the others that if they did mutiny, they would be caught in the toils of mari-time law as soon as they landed and punished with imprison-ment or death. He told them that the sensible way to protest their grievances was to bring legal action against the captain once they were in the United States. The old sailor managed to dampen the revolt. After the *Ronaldson* was back in New York harbor, the crew did prefer charges against Captain Fox, and after due investigation and testimony, the captain was heavily fined.

By that time, Fred was home in Hartford, sleeping in his comfortable bed, eating the good home food of which he had dreamed so long, and then happily roaming out-of-doors, going down familiar roads to visit family and friends who lived around about. He was not forgetting any of the experi-ences of the past year. He would never forget the brutality of the captain. He had first begun to react against harsh and senseless discipline when he was a boy studying with the Rev-erend Brace. Now he hated it totally. Never, for the rest of his life, would he be able to bear the thought of one human exer-cising absolute power over another, and he would fight it whenever he had a chance.

One other thing was clear to him. He did not want a life at sea. He was not going to follow in the wake of his forebears after all, and work his way up from the forecastle to the bridge and the captain's cabin. The sea was glorious in some of its moods. He had seen a few of those. It was terrible in others. He had seen more of those. And he did not want to be a sailor.

So what *was* he going to do?

He talked with his brother, John. He talked with his father. He pondered the problem as he roamed the countryside. What did he like? Well, he liked the out-of-doors, finding pleasure in all the aspects of the countryside.

But what did that add up to? Some sort of career as a naturalist? A botanist? A student of birds, like John James Audubon, who had lectured on natural history in Hartford just a few years before? He could not quite see any of those careers for himself. But there was something much more practical that did seem possible.

Farming! Farmers provided food for themselves and their fellowmen. They lived and worked with nature and could make their farms as beautiful and functional as they pleased. And with all of that, it was a healthy life.

So he made the decision. He would think of farming as a career, and as a first step, he would apprentice himself to some farmer to begin learning the skills of the land.

A FARMER
1844-1847

It was 1844. The much-loved poet, William Cullen Bryant, who was also the editor of the New York *Evening Post*, was beginning to write editorials suggesting that it was time New York City set aside some land for a park. The city was growing so rapidly. There were fewer and fewer open spaces where citizens could stroll quietly under trees. What parks there were, like the Battery, or squares here and there, were much too small to accommodate the throngs of people who would like to enjoy them. Bryant suggested that Jones' Wood, a wild and lovely stretch of land above 60th Street on the east side of Manhattan, should be acquired before it was taken over for small farms and country homes.

A few readers thought about it and nodded in agreement. Among them was a sensitive, beauty-loving young man named Andrew Jackson Downing, who had already won some celebrity for a book he had written on how America's country homes could be improved. He deplored the stark, bare houses built right on the roads. He suggested that the architecture be softened with gables and trellises, that the houses be painted in muted colors that harmonized with nature, and above all, that their grounds should be planted with shrubs and trees in pleasing patterns. He lived up the Hudson River in Newburgh, New York, and he was a landscape gardener by profession, advising some of the wealthy descendants of the Dutch patroons who lived in the Hudson valley on how to plant their estates. Downing was very much interested in the idea of a park for New York City and wrote about the suggestion in a little magazine he published called *The Horticulturalist.*

If Fred was paying any attention to any of this, he gave no sign. He was on his way to being a farmer. For part of one winter, he worked on a farm in southern Connecticut where there was little to do but chop wood and roam the countryside. The next summer he found another job with a farmer near Waterbury, where the work was somewhat more demanding.

Really buckling down to it, he decided to go with John to New Haven that fall, and sit in on some classes on scientific farming at Yale, especially the ones taught by the famous Benjamin Silliman. He enjoyed this brief stay in college. The classes he attended were interesting. He liked the friendliness of dormitory life, the long arguments far into the night with his brother and Charley Brace and other young men, when they discussed all manner of things, but chiefly religion, since religion and the need for conversion were the stylish topics that year.

Best of all were the social evenings with various New Haven families, where the young men could meet young women. On one such evening, Fred met a young woman who had a wonderfully tonic effect on him. For some time he had been half falling in love with any young lady he met. Dazzled by curls and bright eyes and flirting fans, he had done his best to make the proper compliments and act the proper beau. But this young lady, Elizabeth Baldwin, was different. She talked to him seriously, asking about his interests and listening intelligently. He was used to apologizing for being half-educated and for still not having a definite goal. But Miss Baldwin, as he called her, did not think he was so poorly educated and she seemed to understand him when he said he loved the moods of nature. This did not seem strange to her. He loved nature as a poet or an artist would, she said, and she told him of various writers who had the same view of nature and urged him to read the books of Ralph Waldo Emerson and the English writer, John Ruskin.

No romance blossomed, but Fred would remember Miss Baldwin all his life as a young woman who made him think he really would amount to something some day.

His plan for the summer of 1846 was to work on some farm in upper New York State. He took a Hudson River steamboat to Albany and there went to the office of a man who ran a farm paper, hoping to get some suggestions. He got these and also had the opportunity to meet Andrew Jackson Downing. Downing was interested in his plan to become a scientific farmer while at the same time he beautified the land. Fred was pleased by this meeting and with Downing's encouragement.

A few days later, he was settling in at the farm of George Geddes in Onondaga County, to which he had been recommended, and beginning a summer of farm work in the lush fields of northern New York. He liked the work and admired the rich countryside. But somehow he kept remembering a small deserted farm he had discovered the year before on the Connecticut shore. It was on a point of land called Sachem's

Head, a name that memorialized an Indian chief killed long ago in the war between Connecticut settlers and the Pequot Indians. Ploughing and harrowing beside George Geddes, he thought about that little farm and how he might bring it back to life. He talked to Mr. Geddes about it. He wrote to his father about it. Finally, after the harvest was over, he persuaded Mr. Geddes to go to Hartford with him, and then accompany him and his father to look at the farm at Sachem's Head.

It was a lonely place, much run-down. The little brown frame house was in poor repair. The barn was worse, almost falling down. Many of the acres had not been ploughed for years. But the property was directly on the coast and had wonderful views of Long Island Sound. Fred's imagination was busy as he and his father and Mr. Geddes walked about. He saw the lawn he would make in front of the house with a half-circle of low shrubbery sweeping down to the shore. Seeing it as it might be, Fred was so enthusiastic that he soon persuaded his father to buy it for him.

All through the winter he made his plans for it—his own farm at Sachem's Head. He made lists of tools he would need and collected unused furniture from the attic and the barn at Hartford, and at the first breath of spring he was off to start work.

All through the spring and summer, Fred was happily at work with various hired men. They repaired the house, graded the grounds in front of it, set out plants and vines to make the house and its surroundings more attractive. They also ploughed the fields and planted crops of potatoes, vegetables, corn, hay, and barley. They repaired the barn and Fred bought a cow and a few chickens.

And then, somehow, there was not really so much to do. John came for a visit. He and Fred sat on the porch and talked—about religion and politics and girls. There was a summer hotel nearby and they became acquainted with various pleasant people who were guests. And then John went back to Hartford and to Yale. Fred was alone with one hired man and his family and the little farm. He busied himself for a while with his plans for the next year. He looked for cattle to buy and visited nurseries for fruit tree seedlings.

At home in Hartford when all the family gathered for the Thanksgiving feast, he talked to his father about further plans for Sachem's Head. But soon he began to talk about a farm he had seen the year before when he had been visiting on Staten Island—that large, half-deserted island in New York harbor, south of Manhattan's tip. The farm he had seen there was much larger than the little place at Sachem's Head. It was beautifully situated on a high shelf of coastland overlooking all the busy sea traffic of New York Bay. The farm already had orchards and other trees. The house was in fine condition.

John Olmsted listened and sighed. His eyes were puzzled. When would his oldest son find what he was really looking for? Still, he agreed that the Staten Island farm could be investigated. He thought the price that Fred had heard was being asked was rather high. If Fred went to look at the farm he should make sure that there was good water on the land and if tools and stock went with the sale.

A few weeks later, Fred and John traveled south to New York and then ferried across to Staten Island. They went through the house, tramped around the land, and were dazzled by the views from every part of the property.

Home again, Fred reported his excited reactions. Soon his father made the trip to Staten Island with him, and not long after that purchased the Staten Island farm for $13,000. Fred was moving on again.

CHANGES
1848-1850

These were the years when the nation was moving westward in a great tide of settlers and wagons and soldiers and, finally, gold seekers. Texas had been annexed to the United States for a while, then reclaimed by Mexico, then won back to the Union after a brief, feverish war. The flag had gone even farther west and north, and the Oregon Territory was part of the nation.

And with all this push and rush westward went the great question of slavery. Southerners were insisting that slavery followed the flag. Northerners, who had worked out a different system of getting labor to work the land, resisted any spread of slavery. Both groups cried that it was a moral issue. Southerners insisted that some races were born to be slaves and that a fine civilization required slavery as a base. Most Northerners took the stand that it was morally wrong for any human to hold another as a piece of property. But their sug-

gestions varied as to how slavery should be ended. Some insisted that all slavery should simply be abolished at once.
They were the Abolitionists. Others were for more gradual
methods. Some of these thought blacks should be helped to
return to their homeland of Africa. Others thought this was
impractical, and besides, for many blacks, America was their
homeland. They worried about ways of preparing blacks for
freedom and of educating white Southerners to another system of working their land and living their lives.

Fred, his brother John, and their friend, Charles Brace,
discussed the problem night after night, out on the lawn of
the farm at Staten Island, or cosily inside, in the big kitchen.
They were all against slavery and never argued that it should
not be ended somehow. The question was *how*. They raised
their voices and shouted at each other. They quieted and
looked up books that proved some point or another. They
argued the points and finally went to bed exhausted.

Meantime, Fred was employing a variety of workmen to
help him improve his new farm. His first thought, as at
Sachem's Head, was to make the surroundings more attractive. So he and the men worked from sunup to sundown moving the barns and sheds farther from the house. Once these
were concealed behind a little knoll, the aspect of the house
was more pleasing. They worked to move the drive, which
had led straight in from the road, to follow a gentle curve
toward the house and away again. And they planted small
trees and shrubs along the new drive. They drained a swampy
pond back of the house where the cattle had been watered, set
in new pipes, put turf around its banks, and then set out
water plants on the new pond. With all this improving, Fred
did not neglect the regular farm planting of hay, potatoes,
vegetables, and the like. And he studied the peach trees in the
orchard, hoping for a good crop of fruit to sell in New York

by summer's end.

The days passed swiftly. Aunt Maria came from Hartford to take charge of the housekeeping and the cooking. John visited for weeks at a time and Charley Brace came frequently. Fred met some good neighbors, Dr. Perkins, a retired medical professor, and his wife, and their seventeen-year-old granddaughter, Mary. Both Fred and John admired Mary, who was small, pretty, and lively, but John, who was recovering from another illness, had more time than Fred to spend with her.

Fred was introduced to some of a farmer's disappointments in the fall. His peach crop had been splendid, but it had been such a good year for peaches everywhere that the New York market was glutted. As bushels of his peaches rotted, he planned to begin planting pear trees. Perhaps they might be a more profitable crop.

Through the winter, Fred involved himself in local community affairs. The Staten Island farm, which he called Tosomock Farm, was becoming home to him. And when spring came, he rejoiced in the lively, sturdy green of last year's plantings.

John Olmsted, Sr. came out to the farm, with various of his younger children, to spend time during the summer, and he looked about him with satisfaction. Fred was doing well. Surely here, in this comfortable old stone house, with acres of thriving crops around it, Fred was finally settling down, finding the work he had sought so long.

Fred thought this was true himself. He sent his crops to market in the fall and was not displeased with the way they sold. He was full of new projects for the spring.

Visiting the family in Hartford at Thanksgiving, he was not especially surprised when John announced that he and young Mary Perkins were engaged to be married. Perhaps

Fred was a little disturbed to realize that he, twenty-eight now, still had not found a young woman with whom he could share love. However, he *had* become acquainted with another young lady named Perkins—Emily, no relation to Mary, but the daughter of Thomas and Mary Beecher Perkins of Hartford, and the niece of Harriet Beecher Stowe. Thinking about Emily's pretty, intelligent ways and her pleasant manner toward him, he could be generous in his congratulations to his brother and say he would be happy to have Mary as a sister.

But John had another piece of news that was more upsetting. Before making any definite wedding plans, John and Charley Brace were going on a walking tour of England, chiefly for the benefit of John's health. A walking tour of England! Suddenly, Fred realized that this was a trip that he had been wanting to make all his life—certainly since the days when he had first studied the books on English landscapes in his father's library. England was a country that he had dreamed of seeing. It was a country he really needed to see, he thought, if he were to be as good a farmer as he wished.

He waited until he was back at Tosomock Farm, and then wrote a long letter to his father, outlining all those arguments, along with a few more which occurred to him. He suggested that his experiences at sea and in roughing it in general would make him helpful to John and Charley who were not so experienced. He wrote that he could watch over John's health and make sure that he did not overdo or tire himself. In light of all this, he asked his father for one more generous favor. Would he please send him to England along with John?

When the answer came, John Olmsted, Sr. showed himself as loving and sympathetic as always. On consideration, he had decided that it would be a good idea for Fred to go along with John. He could watch over John's health and the trip might improve Fred's own health as well. Along with all this, John Olmsted offered to come to Staten Island during the summer and supervise the farm during Fred's absence.

At once, Fred flew into a frenzy of planning. He talked to everyone he knew who had traveled in England who might help him plan the most rewarding tour that three young men could make on foot. He posted off one letter after another to John and Charley. He hurried to New York to consult Charley in person, and to Hartford to talk with John. There was so much they had to plan. Since they would often be carrying their possessions on their backs, they must think carefully about what was essential. They must decide on what ship they would take, how much they could spend, and make arrangements for the most decent accommodations possible.

They decided at last to sail "second-cabin passage" on an English packet ship, which meant that they could engage a stateroom, and by bringing on board their own food and provisions and hiring their cooking done by the ship's cook, they could make the passage to England for twenty to thirty dollars.

Later, when the great adventure was over, Fred would write some notes for other travelers who wanted to make the European trip at a low cost. He suggested the second cabin, rather than the first, which cost four times as much, but told would-be travelers that they must provide themselves with bedding and cooking utensils as well as food. He suggested that they get berths near the hatchway, wear old clothes, look out for pilferers, be ready to spend an hour each morning in sweeping and keeping clean the area around them, and be prepared also to nurse the sick and look out for women and children. He said that the voyage would probably make them very miserable but it would be over after a while. He mentioned the screw-steamers, which were just coming into use on the ocean, and wrote that one could travel more quickly by them, for from fifty to seventy-five dollars. His feeling was that one would be just as miserable, but that the journey would be over sooner.

But that was hindsight. In April of 1850, Fred, John, and Charley were not dreaming of any miseries. They had their India-rubber army knapsacks and the harnesses for them. Each had filled his knapsack with four shirts, cloth pantaloons, two pairs of socks, slippers, handkerchiefs, mending materials, toilet articles, towel, napkin, leather drinking cup, cap, oil-silk cape, knife and fork, candle, matches, a book, pocket compass, adhesive plaster, cord, shoelacings. And they had all, being observant and studious young men, included writing and sketching materials.

With the knapsacks crammed, and with the food, cooking utensils, and bedding needed for the voyage packed in appropriate boxes, they boarded the *Henry Clay* on April 26, 1850, Fred's twenty-eighth birthday, eager for the voyage that they had been told would not take more than sixteen days.

There was a delay as soon as they boarded. No one seemed to know why. The captain was not aboard to explain and so the passengers muttered and the crew became so restless that a few sailors were talking mutiny. Fred, veteran of a year at sea, sensed the mood, and suggested to the mate that tempers might be eased if someone could play a fiddle for dancing and if a good supper were served to the crew. His suggestions were followed. The tension grew less. At last the captain came aboard, flew into the sort of rage that Fred remembered from the *Ronaldson*, and got every man to his post. Finally, the ship was under way.

Once at sea, life settled into a routine. The quarters which Fred, John, and Charley shared were roomy enough for some comfort. Their food, delivered to the ship's cook, was prepared very well. None of the three suffered long with seasickness. So they roamed the ship, got acquainted with the other passengers, talked a good deal about the wind and weather, watched for whales, played chess with pieces they made themselves out of paper and cork, and joined in the fun when a musical passenger played the fiddle for dancing.

What with the delay in taking off and other setbacks, the voyage took much longer than expected. But finally land was sighted and the ship came into Liverpool harbor. Fred, John, and Charley were so eager to be on land that they left their luggage and backpacks to be brought ashore later and took a little steam-tub to the quay.

And there they were in England! Fred gazed about him, all his senses sharpened. Everything was strange, and yet familiar too. The illustrations that he had studied in his father's books and in the magazines that came from England had all prepared him. Books and poems had painted pictures in his imagination. As he stepped off the tug onto the quay he saw a policeman and recognized him at once as an *English* policeman, from pictures he had seen in the magazine *Punch*. He could hardly wait for the further sights that lay ahead.

ENGLAND
1850

"There we were right in the midst of it! The country—and such a country!—green, dripping, glistening, gorgeous. We stood dumbstricken by its loveliness, as from the bleak and bare boughs we had left at home, broke upon us that English May—sunny, leafy, blooming May—in an English lane; with hedges, English hedges, hawthorn hedges all in blossom. . . ."

He was writing home after he, John, and Charley had begun the first stage of their walking tour. All three of them were enraptured. "No longer excited by daring to think we should see it, as we discussed the scheme around the old home-fire; no longer cheering ourselves with it in the stupid, tedious ship. . . . But there we were, right in the midst of it; long time silent, and then speaking softly, as if it were enchantment indeed. . . ."

A good many Americans were abroad in England that spring and summer. Among them was the landscape gardener,

Andrew Jackson Downing from Newburgh, New York, who was studying English landscapes and looking for a young architect to come into partnership with him. Before the summer was over he found the partner he wanted, a handsome and talented young Englishman, Calvert Vaux. Fred and John and Charley had no thought about other Americans in England, and it would be several years before Fred and Vaux met—in America.

The three young men were simply pilgrims, and for the first few days they were content just to walk, to gaze, and to stop at twilight at some small village inn. Coming from the United States, a country so recently settled, they were entranced by the age of everything they saw. Fred noticed a house with the date 1630 marked on its lintel and recalled that it was in 1636 that one of his ancestors had accompanied Thomas Hooker into the wilds of the Connecticut territory to start the settlement of Hartford. All the old houses and buildings had a mellowness about them unlike anything the young men knew at home. The landscapes had a similar softness. For centuries, English men, women, and children had been living in these dwellings, caring for them, planting the gardens around them, tending the vines and trees, till buildings and landscapes seemed to merge in natural but cultivated shapes.

"We cannot keep still, but run about with boyish excitement," Fred wrote one night in his journal. "We feel indeed like children that have come back to visit the paternal house, and who are rummaging about in the garret among their father's playthings, ever and anon shouting, 'See what I've found! see what I've found!' "

Fred, of course, had talked a great deal about how he was going to study farming methods in England, and almost at once he began to do just that. He stopped at farms, talked with farmers and laborers whenever he could, and constantly observed agricultural details. At night, he wrote long notes in his journal, reporting on the kinds of soil he saw in various districts, the way the land was tilled, the kinds of crops that grew well or poorly, the sort of livestock that was raised. He compared the prices of farm needs with those of the United States. He studied the ways hay was stored, the way cheese was made in Cheshire, and the various methods used for draining the land. Sometimes, so that he could follow his special interests more closely, he separated from John and Charley for a few days and struck off across the countryside on his own, meeting them later at some agreed town.

He did not approve of everything that he saw and made notes on what displeased or shocked him. He discovered that farm laborers in England were paid less than hired laborers in America and that their lives were much harder and more brutish. He found the slums in the few cities that he visited to be much more dismal than the slums in the United States. Making his own deductions, he concluded that it was a great fault of the English ruling classes that they felt no responsibility for the poor or unfortunate among them. Fred, brought up on the words of the American Declaration of Independence, was sure that everyone was born with the same natural rights and should have the same opportunities for education and self-improvement. He could not believe, as many Englishmen seemed to, that some classes of people were born to be poor, miserable, and virtually enslaved.

But in spite of the faults he noted (and after all, America had her faults—black people were still in slavery in the "land of the free"), he continued to feel the same enchantment as when he landed. Here and there, he was able to visit the private park of some nobleman. In such surroundings, he was dazzled by the beauty that could be achieved when men worked carefully and artfully with nature.

"What artist so noble," he wrote later, "as he who, with far-reaching conception of beauty and designing power, sketches the outline, writes the colors, and directs the shadows of a picture so great that Nature shall be employed upon it for generations, before the work he has arranged for her shall realize his intentions."

He had no idea when he wrote this that he was putting into words a description of the profession he would one day make his own, that of an artist . . . sketching the outline, writing the colors, directing the shadows of a picture on which Nature would be employed for generations.

Along with John and Charley, he also visited the public parks in various towns and cities. As public parks did not exist in the United States, Fred observed everything carefully whenever he entered one. They visited New Park, in Birkenhead, near Liverpool, which impressed Fred so much he was willing to admit that "in democratic America there was nothing to be thought of as comparable with this People's Garden." He wrote in his journal of the perfection of the gardening, of the winding paths over acres of a constantly varying surface. He wrote of open fields left grassy for games and sports such as cricket and archery. He wrote of lakes, bridges, summerhouses and roads for carriages that ran through the grounds. "And all this magnificent pleasure ground is entirely, unreservedly, and for ever, the people's own. The poorest British peasant is as free to enjoy it in all its parts as the British queen. More than that, the baker of Birkenhead has the pride of an OWNER in it."

"Is it not a grand, good thing?" he wrote in a letter home. "But you are inquiring who paid for it. The honest owners—the most wise and worthy townspeople of Birkenhead—in the same way that the New Yorkers pay for 'the Tombs,' and the Hospital, and the *cleaning* (as they say) of their streets."

In his own mind, he was still a farmer, or "yeoman," as he had discovered a landowner who farmed his own acres was called in England. As a yeoman, he continued his notes on the rotation of crops, the use of bone for fertilizer, and again and again, the merits of proper drainage.

The three young men were almost a month on their walking tour before their itinerary through southwestern England led them eastward to London. There they visited the landmarks of which they had heard since their childhood—London Bridge, St. Paul's Cathedral, Westminster Abbey. There also, they picked up letters from home—letters from John Olmsted and the rest of the family. John smiled as he read a packet of letters from Mary Perkins, and Charley had his share of mail also.

They took off on a channel boat for the Continent to spend another month in France, Holland, Belgium, and Germany. If Fred did not take quite as many notes in these countries as he had in England, he was still storing up impressions as busily as ever.

Returned to England, they walked across the island to the western coast where they boarded a ship for Ireland. In Ireland, they were shocked by the poverty of the farmers and charmed by their good humor and hospitality. From Belfast, they sailed for Scotland, where they did more walking and sightseeing. But by now, Fred and John were growing weary. Charley, eager for more traveling, decided to go on alone to Germany and Austria. Fred and John said good-bye to him, then journeyed to Glasgow, where they booked passage for America aboard the *City of Glasgow*.

They sailed on October 6, 1850, and the voyage home was very like the voyage out had been—a little stormier, a little more crowded, but finally, just as boring. As before, Fred comforted John with the thought that it would "be over after a while." And weary and bored, he lay awake in his bunk at night and comforted himself with the visions that would never leave him.

He recalled English landscapes with "long, graceful lines of deep green hedges and hedge-row timber, crossing hill, valley and plain in every direction . . . and occasional large trees, dotting the broad fields." He recalled a different light in England, "a much milder light . . . than an American, making the distances and shady parts more indistinct . . ." He had visions of landscapes not especially notable, neither celebrated nor grand, which yet charmed him and soothed him, "full of convenience of man's occupation," and picturesque without striving or ostentation.

WRITER
1850-1851

In the fall of 1850, New Yorkers were going to the polls to elect a new mayor. And thanks to continuing editorials by William Cullen Bryant in the *Post,* and various articles by Andrew Jackson Downing, most of them had become convinced that their city did indeed need a park. As a result, both candidates for mayor had announced they were in favor of such a project. And a few months after the election, the winning candidate, Ambrose Kingsland, was urging the Common Council of the city to proceed at once to acquire the tract known as Jones' Wood for the purpose of making it a park. There were some objections to this proposal, but mostly from people like Andrew Jackson Downing, who thought the site was too small and that a larger, more central tract should be acquired. Whatever the objections, however, the project of a park for New York was definitely under way.

Fred read about it all, of course, and was pleased, but he

never thought of it as concerning him in any way. The news that really agitated him was the passage of the Fugitive Slave Act. The quarreling between the North and the South over the question of slavery had reached a new crisis (it seemed to reach one every few years) when California, thronging with new settlers who had rushed there for gold, asked Congress to be admitted to the Union—as a free state. Southerners were outraged at the idea of another free state in the Union. To mollify them and still admit California, Congress had passed a harsh new law about the capture of runaway slaves. Any white persons helping blacks escape from bondage in the South were subject to severe penalties. Federal officers were authorized to seize black people anywhere and anytime on the suspicion that they might not be free, and no black person could testify in his own behalf. Southerners in general were not especially grateful and thought the law was long overdue. Northerners in general were, like Fred, horrified by the law's cruelty. The nation's most famous minister, Henry Ward Beecher, was preaching disobedience to the law. The minister's sister, Harriet Beecher Stowe, up in Brunswick, Maine, was compulsively writing a novel inspired by her horror of the law. Hundreds of others were protesting in their own ways.

But shocked and horrified as Fred was, he did not see any way in which he could help with his protests. The farm had done well enough during the summer under his father's supervision but with the coming of winter there were hundreds of details that needed attention.

Along with the farm work, he had another project as well. Like many returned travelers, he was struck with a great desire to write about his experiences, and make use of all his pages of notes. He was encouraged in this idea by one of his Staten Island neighbors, George Palmer Putnam, an enterprising New York publisher. If Fred could make a book out of his travels, Putnam said, he would certainly be interested in publishing it.

So Fred asked for his letters from everyone to whom he had written while abroad and began to match them with his notes and to start on a book. As he went over the material, he saw that there were also possibilities for articles in the notes, and he began to plan an article on the park at Birkenhead, which he thought might interest Andrew Jackson Downing for his magazine, *The Horticulturist*.

All through the winter he was happily absorbed in writing. He found it much more satisfying than going about the farm chores which repeated themselves day after day. In the spring, he took time to see about the arrival of a shipment of trees he had ordered abroad. He managed to sell most of them at a good profit, and planted the others. Then he went back to his writing. He sent off the article on the park to Downing and was gratified to hear from Downing a few weeks later that he was going to publish it. He decided to take a trip up the Hudson to Newburgh sometime in the summer to visit Downing and discuss the possibilities of other articles for him. Meantime, he plugged along at the book which he was calling *Walks and Talks of an American Farmer in England*.

The scare about his brother John's health came in early August. John was working during the summer as an interne at a hospital for sailors on Staten Island and he and Mary were planning to be married at the end of the month. Then John suddenly suffered a lung hemorrhage. Everyone was terrified. What John Olmsted, Sr. had always feared about John's health was true. He did have tuberculosis.

Various doctors were consulted. There was talk of postponing John's marriage to Mary. But finally, when John seemed to be mending well, the doctors said that they saw no reason why he should not recover completely, and live to a ripe old age. He and Mary decided to go ahead with their wedding plans, simply postponing the date till October.

After hearing this news, Fred left for Hartford. Inspired by his relief about John's recovery, and perhaps also by the romantic aura around the engaged couple, he went to see Emily Perkins, managed to propose marriage, and was accepted. Somewhat dazed, he returned to Staten Island. At last it had happened. He was engaged to be married, to "the noblest and most sensible woman I ever saw," he wrote.

A farmer, a writer, and now an engaged man. He was trying to realize he was all those things when a letter came from Mrs. Perkins, Emily's mother, begging Frederick to excuse her daughter from the engagement.

Fred could hardly believe it. He hurried back to Hartford to ask Emily what had happened, to plead with her to change her mind, to plead with her family to reason with her. But it was no use. Emily, it seemed, had recently met a handsome young minister, Edward Everett Hale (who would win fame one day as an author), and the fondness she had for Fred was overwhelmed by the love she felt for this new suitor.

When Fred came back to the farm, everyone spoke and walked softly, expecting him to be heartbroken. He looked solemn and said that he was crushed. But after a few days he seemed to recover. Perhaps he was secretly relieved that Emily had ended an engagement that he was not so eager for as he had thought.

Certainly he was cheerful enough for John's wedding to Mary which took place October 16. Then he and all the family went to see the newlyweds off on a ship to Europe, where they were going to look for some place with a climate that would benefit John's health.

After that, Fred returned to finishing *Walks and Talks of*

an American Farmer, and supervising the management of the farm. Charley Brace, back from Europe, visited him from time to time, and sometimes brought with him such well-known Abolitionists as William Lloyd Garrison or Theodore Parker. When such guests were present, the talk went on far into the night. Charley, Parker, and Garrison all insisted that slavery must be abolished immediately. Fred, hating the system as much as they did, could not help taking a longer view. He argued that black people who had been kept so long in subjection and ignorance needed to be educated and prepared for freedom. He thought it was the responsibility of slaveowners to see that the black people whom they had enslaved were given those advantages before they were asked to make their own way in the world. The others scoffed at him, asking if he thought it likely that any slaveowners would assume such a responsibility. But Fred held doggedly to his own views.

Sometimes he enjoyed social evenings at George Palmer Putnam's house, acting in amateur theatricals or joining in literary discussions. When Palmer moved across the bay into New York, Fred continued to visit him. Every Tuesday evening Palmer had an open house for New York literary figures and Fred liked to go to these gatherings and meet such celebrities as William Cullen Bryant, Bayard Taylor, and that most famous of American writers, Washington Irving.

By late fall Fred had finished *Walks and Talks* and Putnam had accepted it. Fred did not expect to make much money from the book, for Putnam was publishing it as part of a new series of paperbound books which were to be sold so cheaply that everyone could afford them. Still, Fred looked forward to the publication of his first book in February, 1852, hoping that what he had written about the landscaping beauties of England might have at least some effect on American taste.

When the reviews of his book began to appear he was happily surprised. Mr. Downing had kind things to say about it in *The Horticulturist*, and to Fred this meant praise from a master. There were friendly reviews in other magazines. And indeed, it was a good and pleasant book. Informally written, it reflected the happiness and wonder Fred had felt as he traveled, but it did not avoid any of the serious considerations of human poverty and misery either, and Fred's own suggestions for their remedies.

Once again, Fred was sure he had found his place in life—managing his farm and writing books and articles on subjects that had to do with farming and the land.

And so, very soon, he was offered an irresistible opportunity to change his course—and this time, the opportunity offered him a chance to really do something in the struggle against slavery.

REPORTER
ON SLAVERY
1851-1853

"The filly was just so pleasantly playful and full of well-bred life as to create a joyful, healthy, sympathetic, frolic-some heedlessness in her rider—walking rapidly, and with a some-times irresistible inclination to dance and bound; making be-lieve she was frightened at all the burnt stumps, and flashes of sunlight on the ice, and every time a hog lifted himself up before her, starting back in the most ridiculous manner, as if she had never seen a hog before, bounding over the fallen trees as easily as a lifeboat over a billow . . . and yet never failing to answer to every motion of my hand or knees as if she were part of myself. In fact, there soon came to be a real good understanding . . . between Jane and me . . ."

Where was Fred now? Actually, he was not too sure him-self. He was a little bit lost, somewhere south of Richmond in rural Virginia, riding a rented filly named Jane Gillin, and looking for the home of a planter who lived somewhere in the area. And why was he looking for this planter? Because he was embarked on a reporting project that was to take him over most of the cotton states of the South where slavery was held to be a necessary fact of life.

He owed the assignment partly to the success of his book, *Walks and Talks*, and partly to the recommendation of his friend, Charley Brace. Charley knew Henry Raymond, the editor of one of New York's many newspapers, *The New York Times*. Talking one day with Raymond about their mutual hatred of slavery, Charley mentioned the great impact that Mrs. Stowe's book, *Uncle Tom's Cabin*, was having. Raymond said that if the book had any fault, it appealed too much to the emotions. He wished that someone would travel about the South and report on slavery as it was, without any emotional bias, simply describing how things were in the slave states. Charley mentioned that his friend, Frederick Olmsted, had recently done just that sort of reporting on a trip they had taken to England. Raymond knew the book, *Walks and Talks*. He wondered if Olmsted would be interested in making a tour of the slave states and writing a series of letters about his observations for the *Times*. Charley thought he might be. Soon after that, Mr. Raymond wrote to Fred. Fred went in to the city to talk to him.

And so, by the middle of December, 1852, Fred was on his way, going first to Washington, D.C., from there to Richmond, and then planning to travel by various means through Virginia, North Carolina, Georgia, and Alabama.

One of the chief means of travel, of course, in areas where railway cars did not reach, was horseback, so there he was, on his rented filly, Jane, ambling along through the countryside of Virginia on a bright December day. They passed pine groves, deserted log cabins, more pine groves, and "old fields," which were fields that had been in cultivation until the soil had become useless and was abandoned. They had passed no cows or sheep, only hogs, wild ones, which came dashing across their path in packs with short, nasty grunts. But they saw no landmarks that signaled an approach to the planter's home.

"Never mind," said Jane, lifting her head and turning in the direction they had been going. "I don't think it's any great matter if we are lost, such a fine day—."

"Very well, my dear," answered Fred. "You know the country better than I do; go where you like . . . It's evident we are not going straight to Mr. W.'s; I'll try at least to take note of what we do pass after this . . ."

So he talked to the filly and imagined her remarks and enjoyed himself. He had always had an easy way with horses —dogs too—respecting the unique personality in each creature. Perhaps it was this ability to see what was unique in all things—trees, plants, even rocks, as well as people and animals—that made him a good reporter.

Later, he wrote about the various places at which he had stopped, seeking directions to "Mr. W.'s." He described the lonely, ramshackle cabins and their inhabitants, both white and black, and their confused and ignorant responses. Nobody, it seemed, had any notion of local geography beyond a mile or so from where he lived. "Go back to the Court House," one man finally said, "and they'll tell you there." So Fred rode a mile or so to a tiny town, with a plain brick building which he realized was the Court House. He stopped at a frame building labeled "Hotel," and had his lunch while Jane had corn and fodder in the barn. Then he and Jane set forth again with a new set of directions.

He wrote about it all in his letter to the *Times*, and it was not just an aimless story of being lost, but a picture of the rural South, indolent, ignorant, isolated. He wrote about seeking shelter for the night in the home of a churlish farmer. He described the dinner he was served, with five different sorts of hot breads, and he wrote about the slaves who were part of even this poor establishment. After dinner, he managed to get his host to talk about farming practices in the area.

No, the farmer said, white men did not hire out as farm laborers in the South. That was work for "niggers." True, the slaves were slow, but they were "reliable—you could command them and *make* them do what was right."

The next day, Fred took off again in search of the planter, "Mr. W.," and this time he found his goal. He entered the rather lavish establishment of a wealthy tobacco planter. The house was an old family mansion remodeled in the Grecian style. Mr. W. was a gracious host, eager to entertain him. Fred wrote of the dinner he had here, the dishes of "fried fowls, fried eggs, cold roast turkey, and opossum," and one vegetable, "sweet potato, roasted in ashes." He wrote of the young black children and the hound dogs who clustered around everyone's seat throughout the meal. And he wrote of his conversations with Mr. W. about labor in the South. Mr. W. had been hiring some white laborers to do some drainage work for him, and did not think they worked as well as Negroes. Then why had he used them? Because the work was unhealthy and Negroes were too expensive to expose to unhealthy conditions. At the same time, Mr. W. said that "his negroes never worked so hard as to tire themselves . . . He did not think they ever did half a fair day's work. They could not be made to work hard."

Mr. W. pressed Fred to stay for several days but Fred had further engagements farther south, so he left with Jane the next morning, to return Jane to her home stable. After leaving her ("I am sorry to say she appeared very indifferent"),

Fred made his way to the little railroad station, where he learned that the train was always likely to be half an hour behind its advertised time if it were not half an hour ahead.

So he went on with his travels and his visits, his conversations and his observations. He wrote quietly of what he saw and heard, painting pictures of the scenes and the people he encountered, with no attempt to introduce his own point of view. And gradually, though he reported all sorts of opinions by white men defending slavery, a few by men who did not approve of it, and various conversations that he had with slaves, one larger picture began to emerge out of all the smaller ones. Whatever each individual said, slavery showed itself as a wasteful way of working the land. Slaves, provided with the minimum necessities of life, and with no hope of improving their lives by their own efforts, were mostly unwilling to do more than the minimum required of them. Many shammed illness or actually did themselves some injury so as to escape work. Fred pointed out how this lack of incentive to work affected poorer white people, who would not do the work allotted to blacks and had no respect for what they themselves could do either.

In Louisiana, Fred talked with a slave, a house servant, who seemed happy with his life and fond of his master. He thought his plantation the best in the state. It was the best-worked plantation and made the most sugar. All the blacks had enough to eat, were well clothed, their quarters were good, and they got a good many presents.

"Well now," Fred asked, "wouldn't you rather live on such a plantation than to be free, William?"

The answer came promptly. "Oh! no, sir, I'd rather be free! Oh, yes, sir, I'd like it better to be free; I would dat, master."

"Why would you?"

"Why, you see, master, if I was free—if I was *free*, I'd have *all* my time to myself. I'd rather work for myself. I'd like dat better."

"But then, you know, you'd have to take care of yourself, and you'd get poor."

"No, sir, I would not get poor, I would get rich: for you see, master, then I'd work *all de time* for myself."

Over and over again, Fred let whites and blacks speak for themselves, and made no judgments. The conclusions then spoke for themselves. The whites had deliberately reduced blacks as nearly as they could to the status of owned animals. They gave them no opportunities to learn how to manage their own lives, and then justified keeping them in slavery by saying that they were an inferior race.

After miles of traveling, listening, and recording his observations, Fred returned to New York in April. By this time, Mr. Raymond had published eight of his letters in the *Times* over the signature of "Yeoman." Fred had notes for thirty or forty more letters and was pleased to hear that Raymond wanted as many as he could write. The "Yeoman" letters were stirring up just the sort of interest Raymond had hoped for. People were putting aside the emotional aspects of the problem, honest and important as those were, and considering how people, white and black, could live and work together sensibly and economically. Of course, many Southern readers of the *Times* felt that no Northerner could be unprejudiced about slavery and that Olmsted should not be trusted. But a surprising number of Southern newspapers wrote that although Olmsted might be prejudiced, he was honest and intelligent.

Back on the Staten Island farm, Fred had to realize that he was still a yeoman as well as a traveling reporter. The planting season was at hand and a thousand details required attention. His fruit trees needed pruning. Repairs were needed on the house and barns. He hurried about the fields and orchards, giving instructions to his workers—hired free men, all of them. Then he went back into the house to his desk and his notes, to write up the rest of the Southern material.

In June, he went in to New York to welcome home John and Mary, returning from their long stay in Europe, and to meet their baby son, his new nephew, John Charles, who had been born the previous September in Geneva, Switzerland. Now Fred could find out for himself if John's health had improved during the European stay and he could hear all about the adventures he and Mary had had in Rome, Switzerland, and elsewhere. He could talk too, about his own adventures in the Southland. And he spoke of his plans to make still another journey, this time into the South and West, particularly Texas, to see how slave labor was being used in a frontier country.

Suddenly, John began to wonder if it might not benefit his health if he joined Fred on this next journey. They might travel all the way to California and see if the climate there was as beneficial as reported. Fred was delighted by the idea. Soon he and John were making definite plans.

By the late fall of 1853, they were saying good-bye to Mary and the baby, to their father and the rest of the family, and were on their way.

ANTI-SLAVERY
AGITATOR
1853-1855

In New York City, the park project was slowly inching along. Everyone had been shocked when one of the project's chief supporters, Andrew Jackson Downing, was drowned in a terrible steamboat explosion on the Hudson River. But the momentum that he and William Cullen Bryant had given to the project was not halted. In fact, because of Downing's complaints that the Jones' Wood tract was too small for a park, a committee was appointed to find a larger, more central site. In due time, the committee fixed on a long, narrow tract of land to the north of the city in the middle of the island. And in further due time, the State Legislature authorized the city to acquire both Jones' Wood and the central site—soon called Central Park.

And then, of course, another board had to be appointed to dicker with the owners of the land on both sites about the purchase prices of their acreages. Still, slow as the process was,

61

something was being done. New York City *would* have a park some day.

Meantime, Fred and John were far away, jogging across Texas. They traveled across the hot, dusty countryside. They found some sort of wretched lodging each night where they could eat some greasy food and lie down on dirty beds. Fred kept making his notes—on the land, the people they met, how they lived. And then came the big surprise.

"I never in my life," Fred wrote, "except perhaps, in awakening from a dream, met with such a sudden and complete transfer of associations. Instead of loose boarded or hewnlog walls with crevices stuffed with rags or daubed with mortar, which we have been accustomed to see during the last month . . . instead, even of four bare cheerless sides of white-washed plaster, which we have found twice or thrice only in a more aristocratic American residence, we were—in short, we were in Germany . . .

"There was nothing wanting; there was nothing too much . . . A long room, extending across the whole front of the cottage, the walls pink, with stenciled panels, and scroll ornaments in crimson . . . neatly framed lithographic prints hanging on all sides; a long, thick, dark oak table, with rounded ends, oak benches at its sides . . . a sofa . . . a stove in the corner; a little mahogany cupboard in another corner . . . and finally, four thick-bearded men . . . who all bow and say 'Good morning,' as we lift our hats in the doorway . . .''

What Fred and John had found was the town of Neu Braunfels in west Texas, and in the next day or so they heard something of its history. It had been settled some ten years before by German immigrants, most of them well-educated men and women, fleeing Germany for political reasons. The settlers had known extreme hardship after their arrival, but gradually, those who survived managed by determination and hard work to turn the desert into a garden spot—a pleasant town with neat farms surrounding it.

Fred, and John too, became even more impressed when they learned that all this had been done without any use of slave labor. In the midst of a Southern territory where most men were urging the absolute necessity of slavery, here was proof that the best and most profitable use of the land came from free labor.

Fred wrote several letters for the *Times* about Neu Braunfels, before he and John journeyed on to the Mexican border and the Texas coast.

They had to give up their plans for traveling on to California because they could not find a party to join for the trip. In 1854, the overland journey through Indian territory was considered too dangerous to undertake unless with a large group. So they made up for their disappointment in that by returning to the fascinating town of Neu Braunfels which seemed even more attractive on the second visit. Now they became firm friends with some of the leaders of the community and vowed to stay in touch through letters in the future.

At last they were on their way east again. When they reached the Mississippi River, John turned northward to return home. Fred started off on a slower tour of observation through the back country of the South where conditions were quite different from along the seaboard. But finally, Fred too, was back at the farm on Staten Island.

He took a quick, abstracted look around to see how John had managed things after his return, and then he disappeared with his notes and papers to his desk. The farm now seemed the least of his concerns.

What he cared about was slavery and what could be done to stop its spread. While he and John were away, Congress had passed the Kansas-Nebraska Bill which was supposed to settle the long argument as to whether the Nebraska Territory should be admitted to the Union as a free state or a slave state. The solution of Congress had been to divide the territory in two, admit the northern half, Nebraska, as a free state, and let the southern half, Kansas, choose by the vote of its settlers whether it preferred to be for slavery or freedom. Fred knew —everybody knew—what this was going to mean. Kansas was going to become a battleground as pro-slavery people rushed settlers to the area to be ready to vote for slavery, and anti-slavery people hurried people there to vote against it.

Fred hoped that by writing of his own experiences and observations he could convince some people not that slavery was wrong and wicked but that it was against their own self-interest. He wanted to make them see, as he had seen, the contrast between the rough, ramshackle sort of life that followed slavery, and the bright, productive farms and towns he had seen in west Texas, worked by free men.

So he wrote letter after letter, describing Neu Braunfels, trying not only to make the contrast clear between slave economy and a free one, but to encourage people from the East to migrate to west Texas.

More secretly, he became involved in trying to raise funds to send arms to the free settlers in Kansas. For a while, he was often away from the farm, talking to one person after another in New York, asking for contributions to buy guns or cannon.

In what time he had left from these anti-slavery activities, he was writing other articles for the newspapers and magazines. In all of these his concern was with how people could live together more sensibly.

Soon after his return home, two ships had collided in a fog off the Atlantic coast with a terrible loss of life. News of this tragedy had brought back all his memories of his year at sea. He wrote a long article for the *Times* suggesting ways in

Olmsted Associates, Inc.

Frederick Law Olmsted, c. 1860

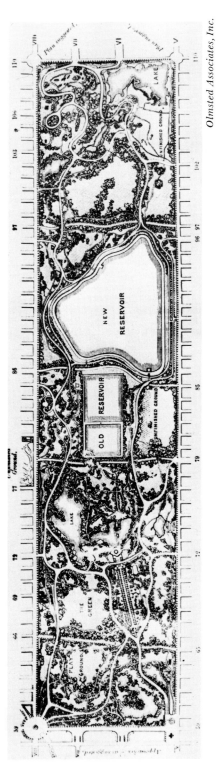

Olmsted Associates, Inc.

First study of design for the Central Park. From a wood-cut made in 1858.

Olmsted Associates, Inc.

Map of the Central Park, 1868

Courtesy of The New York Historical Society, New York City

Central Park as it was in 1862

Calvert Vaux

Olmsted Associates, Inc.

A tree-moving machine of 1868

One of the sunken transverse roadways in Central Park

Olmsted Associates, Inc.

Courtesy of The New York Historical Society, New York City

Olmsted Associates, Inc.

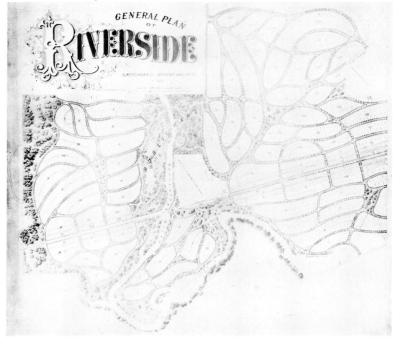

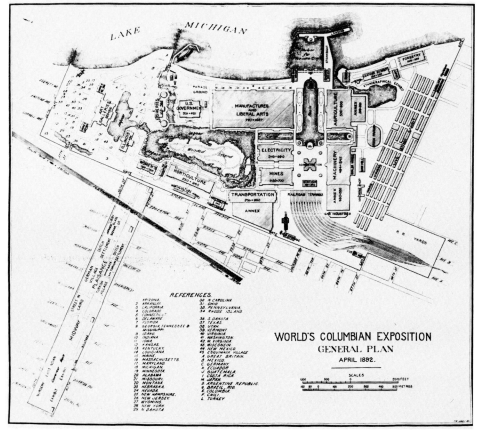

Olmsted Associates, Inc.

Olmsted's plan for the Columbian Exposition in Chicago in 1893

Opposite (top): Prospect Park in Brooklyn, c. 1880

Opposite (bottom): Plan for Riverside Park in Manhattan

West side approaches to the Capitol in Washington, D.C., from an Olmsted perspective drawing

An illustration from Olmsted's book, *A Journey in the Seaboard Slave States,* 1856

A VIRGINIA FARM-HOUSE

which such disasters could be avoided in the future. One suggestion was so practical that it was surprising no one had
made it before. Fred wrote that ships running in a fog should
be required by law to keep firing a signal gun or a steam
whistle so that other ships in the vicinity would be aware of
their presence.

He also wrote about a plan that had been dear to him since
the year on the *Ronaldson*. This was a suggestion that men
and boys be trained for work at sea just as they were trained
for other respectable callings. Such training would make a
body of responsible men available for ships' crews, so that
there would be no need to round up drunks and derelicts to
man vessels. Instead, ships could be manned by men capable
of working in an intelligent, disciplined way. With such crews
there would be no need or excuse for captains who tyrannized
over their men, swinging whips and meting out terrible punishments.

Other problems of the day concerned him as well. More
and more immigrants were crowding into New York, so many
that most of them were unable to find employment. Soup
kitchens were set up to keep these people from starving, but
these did not solve any problem. Prisons and poorhouses were
filled to overflowing. Many thoughtful people had suggested
that these immigrants could find jobs in other parts of the
country. Fred did not stop there. He prepared a question-
naire to be published in newspapers and magazines throughout the country, asking farmers for information about jobs
for hired workers in their areas.

People!—white, black, sailors, immigrants—and how they
could lead better lives—these seemed to have become Fred's
chief concern. He wrote article after article on his suggestions
and findings. And meantime, he was also busy revising his
letters to the *Times* from his first Southern tour so that they

could be published as a book. John, who had taken over most of the management of the farm, spent his spare time helping Fred get the final letters from Texas in shape for publication.

Once again Fred's life seemed to have taken a definite shape and direction. But he was still Frederick Olmsted, of the "truant disposition"—Fred, whose life had veered like a berserk compass needle from his earliest days. So now he went off in still another direction.

He was not turning his back on the problems that concerned him so much. It simply seemed to him that he might have a much wider influence if he carried those concerns into a wider field.

And so, in 1855, he became a magazine editor, and soon, a book publisher as well.

PUBLISHER AND EDITOR 1855-1857

Progress on New York City's park seemed to have stalled. Various real estate developers had managed to prevent the city from acquiring the Jones' Wood tract, but although the large, central site had been acquired, nothing was being done there either. A new mayor, Fernando Wood, had been elected. But his election had been won by so much obvious fraud by Tammany Hall that responsible New Yorkers hesitated to let Mayor Wood and his men have free run of a project like the park. They were sure he would turn it into a grand political pay-off for everyone who had sold a vote to Tammany, and to prevent this, they used every tactic they could to delay work on the park. And so, in 1855, the 840 acres in the center of Manhattan that had been set aside for the project remained as they were—an expanse of swamps, rocky outcroppings, and squatters' shacks. An engineer, Egbert Viele, was hired to make a topographic map of the area. And that was it.

Frederick Olmsted seemed to be paying no attention at all. He was totally involved in his new career. A few years before, his publisher friend, George Putnam, had established *Putnam's Magazine*, which quickly became known for publishing the best American and English writers. When Putnam got into financial difficulties with some of his other ventures, he sold the magazine to two young men, John Augustus Dix and Arthur Edwards. Fred happened to know Dix and learned from him that if he could invest five thousand dollars in the magazine he could become an editor and member of the firm. Once again, as so often before, Fred went to his father. He managed to convince John Olmsted that to become an editor of *Putnam's Magazine* would be a wonderful step for him. He would be in a position to buy or commission articles on all aspects of American life, and to influence American taste and progress in all sorts of ways.

And so, in January, 1855, he moved in to the city to be near his new work. He left his brother John in charge of the farm. John was not well at all and not very interested in farming either, but he and Mary now had two small children. John's health would not allow him to practice medicine and he had to do something. So he sighed and agreed to stay on at the farm until Fred could sell it. And Fred was on his way.

Fred was excited at first by being an editor. He enjoyed meeting writers and talking to them. He was delighted to journey off to Boston and other New England cities to meet such literary lights as Emerson, Longfellow, and Harriet Beecher Stowe. His judgment of articles and stories submitted for publication was generally very good and the magazine continued to be successful.

Business was so good, in fact, that Fred, Dix, and Edwards decided to do some book publishing as well. Among the first books they planned was Fred's almost completed collection of letters from his travels in the seaboard slave states. This was soon in print and receiving very good reviews—in the North. Southern slaveowners were just as angry with a book that showed that slavery was uneconomical as they were with books which said it was inhumane.

Soon Fred was planning a business trip to England. One of his young half sisters, Bertha, was already studying in Paris. Another one, Mary, was anxious to join Bertha and to see a little of Europe with her. Fred arranged to take Mary with him to London, then go to Paris with her to meet Bertha, after which they would all take a quick tour of Italy.

By a freak of fate, the ship on which they sailed ran into a heavy fog when they were a few days out of New York. Everyone remembered the tragic collision in a fog that had taken place a few years ago and a good many passengers remembered Fred's public recommendation that ships in a fog sound continual warnings. The captain of this ship, however, was a bullheaded man and sounded no warnings but steered the ship straight on through the murk. Luck was with him and they came through safely.

In London, Fred called on publishers, trying to convince them to appoint Dix and Edwards the American publishers of their successful English books. He also met with various English authors. Then he and Mary sailed for France, to meet Bertha and set forth on their Italian tour.

Years later, Fred would note in a sort of wonder how he had stored up impressions of Italian landscapes and gardens at a time when he had "no more thought of becoming a landscape architect than a cardinal."

No, he was a publisher now, and was soon hurrying back to London to continue his negotiations there and to see about the English publication of his book, *A Journey Through the Seaboard Slave States*. But a great deal of bad news was waiting for him. Not only was there bad news nationally—a bloody massacre of anti-slavery forces in Kansas by pro-slavery men, and a nearly fatal attack on a United States Senator by an enraged Southern Representative—he had terrible news about his own firm, which Dix wrote was in deep financial trouble. Fred tried to make some sense of the tangle during the next days. He put the problem aside briefly when his father and stepmother arrived to join Mary and Bertha, and then he went back to his worries. Before long he was on his way back to the United States to do what he could to straighten out the affairs of Dix and Edwards, and then—to resign.

Arrived in New York, he went straight to the farm in Staten Island. He was shocked to see John looking very ill. He hid his alarm until John had gone to bed, then he spoke anxiously to Mary. Mary tried to be her usual brisk self but Fred could see that it was not easy. John's health was not good. Neither was the farm doing well. And every attempt to sell it had fallen through.

Worried about John, Fred went to the Dix and Edwards offices to face the troubles there. At first, it appeared that the situation was not so bleak as both Dix and Edwards had painted it when he was in England. Fred settled in again as an editor and worked on another collection of his travel letters from the South, *A Journey in the Back Country*. John, meanwhile, was working up the notes Fred had made of their Texas journey for still another book, *A Journey Through Texas*. Both hoped that this book might lure settlers to free Texas, not only from the United States but from England and Germany as well.

But even as the book *A Journey Through Texas* was being published, Mary was packing trunks for John, herself, and the two children, and making arrangements for a long absence. She and John had decided that they should look for some climate abroad that might help John's health.

Fred said good-bye to them at a Hudson River pier. He looked long at the brother who had been his best friend all his life, and he wondered if he would see John again. He kissed Mary and said good-bye to his small nephew and niece. Then he went back to the publishing company where the troubles were worsening again.

Altogether, it took six months and more before Fred was finally able to end his connection with the unfortunate firm of Dix and Edwards. Soon after he left, the firm went into bankruptcy and one way or another Fred too was responsible for some of the firm's debts.

When he sat at last at his desk in the farmhouse on Staten Island, he could not see how his association with publishing had achieved any of the great aims for which he had hoped. *A Journey Through Texas* had received good reviews and was stirring up conversation here and there but it certainly had not spurred any great migration to the free section of Texas. Fred looked at the papers before him, the nearly completed manuscript of *A Journey Through the Back Country.* He really did not see how that was going to have any effect on the way people acted about slavery either. The same people would read it who had read his other books—people who already believed that slavery was wrong.

He thought about the latest news from John and Mary. They had gone from the West Indies to Paris, from Paris to Italy, where they had met John Olmsted, Sr., who was anxiously awaiting them. Then they had all traveled together to Switzerland, hoping that the climate there might help John. But the latest letter had reported that John's lung hemorrhages were more frequent. He weighed only a hundred pounds and most days he was too weak to rise from his bed.

Fred himself felt a weariness and a hopelessness that he had never felt before. His brother was dying. His own efforts through the years had amounted to nothing. What was the use of fussing any more with this manuscript before him? What was the use of anything he did?

And then, suddenly, he refused to allow himself to despair. Whether it was any use or not, he would finish this last book. And if he could not write here at Tosomock Farm with all its sad memories, he would go somewhere else.

He packed up his manuscript and notes and some clothes and traveled northward and eastward to a small seaside inn in Connecticut. He took a room and sat down to finish the book.

It was there, in that little Connecticut inn, in August, 1857, when he was thirty-seven years old, that Frederick Olmsted finally began to listen seriously to some conversation about the new park being planned for New York City, and began to think seriously that he might have some part in it.

PARK
SUPERINTENDENT
1857

New York City seemed bursting at its seams. Immigrants were still pouring in from Europe, crowding into tiny rooms in decayed tenements, going out to seek vainly for some sort of work. Gangs of hoodlums roamed the streets of the poorer neighborhoods, fighting and killing, and were generally undisturbed by the police who were instructed by Tammany Hall to remember that every tough had a vote to sell. Adding to the misery came a financial panic. Dix and Edwards was not the only firm to fail that year. Many respectable companies were going bankrupt and many men who had always made a good living were wondering desperately how they could provide for their families.

In the midst of this, work on a park for the city's inhabitants was slowly getting under way. To avoid as much political profiteering as possible, a new Board of Commissioners had been appointed which was supposed to be nonpartisan.

To add a further check, still another board was appointed to offer general advice and supervision. Among those on this board were Washington Irving, the historian George Bancroft, and other distinguished citizens. Egbert Viele, who had mapped the acreage purchased for the park and drawn up a plan for it, was named chief engineer and he had begun to hire gangs of men to clear the rough and swampy areas.

Fred had a general knowledge of all this from reading the newspapers. Then, one day, as he was having tea at the seaside inn, he sat beside an acquaintance of his, Charles Elliott, who was one of the commissioners. It was natural for Fred to ask how things were progressing with the park. Mr. Elliott replied that the board was currently looking for a superintendent to supervise the work. They hoped to select one at their next meeting but no one who seemed especially qualified had yet been interviewed.

Fred asked what the superintendent's duties would be. Mr. Elliott replied that he would direct the laborers and generally oversee construction. He said that the board hoped to hire someone who was not a politician. Republicans and Democrats were going to have to cooperate if the park were to be kept free of politics.

Fred said that all seemed sensible and that a park so managed would be a fine thing for New York.

Suddenly Mr. Elliott looked at him and said, "I wish we had you on the commission, but as we have not, why not take the superintendency yourself? Come, now!"

Fred stared. "*I* take it?" he said finally. Then he blinked as if to clear his eyes to a new and astonishing vista. "I'm not sure that I wouldn't—if it were offered to me. Nothing interested me in London like the parks, and yet I thought a great deal more might be made of them."

"Well," said Mr. Elliott, "the post's not going to be offered to you, that's not the way we do business; but if you'll go to work I believe you may get it . . . Go to New York and file an application, see the Commissioners and get your friends to back you."

"I'll take the boat back to New York tonight," Fred said, "and think it out as I go. If no serious objection occurs to me before morning, I'll do it."

He said good-bye to Mr. Elliott, packed up his things, took the boat back to New York, and no serious objection occurred to him.

The next morning he started out to visit one friend after another, asking for an endorsement. In his years as a writer, he had met a great many prominent men. Even those two unhappy years as a publisher had not been wasted, since they had introduced him to a wide circle of important people. One friend wrote a letter for him. Another drew up a petition and had it signed by a number of well-known men, including Washington Irving. Fred wrote a petition himself, outlining his qualifications. He wrote that he was experienced in managing agricultural labor (as indeed he was from his years as a farmer), that he had studied public grounds in England, France, Germany, and Italy, and given special attention to the policing of grounds and the way labor was employed. He easily obtained almost two hundred signatures for this petition, among those who signed being William Cullen Bryant, Whitelaw Reid, and August Belmont.

The board meeting to choose the new superintendent was being held on September 11. Fred learned that four other men were also under consideration and all had qualifications. So he joined a lawyer friend whose office was near the board's meeting place, and tried to calm his nerves by writing to John, in Switzerland.

Finally a messenger came to him. He looked at the mes-

senger's face, read the note, and relaxed. He thanked the messenger and then hurried to add to his letter to John. "After a
very long session and much debate, I am elected; on the final
vote, 8 of those present voting for me and one against me . . .
The strongest objection to me, that I am a literary man, not
active; yet if I had not been a 'literary man' so far, I certainly
should not have stood a chance."

The messenger had told him that Washington Irving's endorsement had been the deciding factor in ending the debate.
If Irving was for Olmsted, no one wanted to argue. And if
Olmsted had not met Irving in his years as a "literary man,"
would Irving have been such an enthusiastic sponsor? So, it
had worked out well, and if some men on the commission still
felt that he was not a "practical man," he would show them.

"Not a practical man . . ." The phrase gradually came to be
a bugaboo to Fred, a remark that he heard so often from
anyone who opposed him on park matters of any nature that
he finally began to call himself defiantly an "*imp*ractical
man," and let the results he achieved speak for themselves.

He was challenged with being impractical when he went to
meet Egbert Viele a few days later, in his small rough offices
near the park grounds. Fred had thought it would be just a
formal visit to meet the man who would be his superior. But
after a few words of greeting, the chief engineer arose and
said briskly, "I suppose you'll want to see what the situation
is." Then he called for one of the foremen who was nearby.
The foreman appeared, his rough trousers tucked into muddy
boots. "This is Mr. Hawkins," Viele said. "*He* is what I call a
practical man."

Fred nodded. Mr. Viele then asked Mr. Hawkins to take
Fred on a tour of the grounds. Mr. Hawkins looked at Fred,
neatly dressed in city clothes.

"Now?" asked Mr. Hawkins doubtfully. Mr. Viele looked
at Fred.

"I am quite ready, sir," said Fred. And off he went after the booted Hawkins, who proceeded to lead him through all the swampiest bogs and up the roughest, most brambly heights in the vicinity. Now and then they both had to stop as Fred tried to scrape some of the mud and slime off his trousers and shoes. Hawkins watched with interest.

"I suppose you are used to this sort of business," Hawkins said, smiling a little. Fred could only look up at him, and then return to his scraping.

In the days that followed, Fred set about showing Mr. Hawkins and the workmen who were currently employed— about four hundred in all—that he was indeed used to this sort of business. Dressed in his rough farm clothing, his trousers tucked into rubber boots, he went from one gang of workmen to another. He saw them leaning on their spades or resting against rocks, their grubbing tools on the ground beside them. He saw them smiling as he approached, sure he was just a city dude who would not know whether they were doing their work or not. The most that they hoped from him was that he would soon promote them to a higher pay bracket to make room for more workmen who were referred by political bosses.

Fred said little as he greeted each group, but what he said had the ring of authority. Shock waves began to spread out among the men. Perhaps this superintendent was not going to be such an easy mark after all. They looked uneasily at one another.

Within a few weeks, they had learned the worst. The new superintendent Olmsted expected a day's work for a day's pay. More than that, he knew what a day's work should be. Olmsted organized the work of clearing, draining, and filling and made it clear to each gang of men when a certain job should be completed.

Fred also began hiring more workmen. It was a difficult

task. Unemployment in the city was increasing as the fall came, and hundreds were clamoring for jobs. But most men came with no other recommendation than a note from their ward chairman, who had promised them some reward for their vote. Eager to hire honest, responsible men who really needed the work, Fred passed over many of those with only political recommendations and so caused a good many more people to think that he was a very impractical man.

Still, under Fred's daily supervision, the work began going well. Since he never hesitated to get down in the muck himself, to swing an axe or to show how roots should be grubbed out, many workmen began to respect him and to work more cheerfully than ever before. Fred's belief that discipline could be a healthy thing when there was mutual respect between those giving the orders and those receiving them was proving correct.

It was good that Fred had this daily demanding activity. As the days grew colder and the leaves began to turn, he had the news from abroad that he had been dreading. John was weakening.

December had come and a few early snows had blown by when he had a letter from John written in early November. John was saying good-bye. He wrote briefly of what their life-long friendship had meant to him. He said that he could hardly comprehend the suddenness of what was happening. Finally he asked Fred not to let Mary suffer while he was alive. "God bless you," he wrote in a trembling hand, and signed his letter "John H.O."

Fred had known the moment was coming. He had tried to prepare himself. Still he was not prepared when another letter came a few weeks later from his father, telling him that John had died November 24, 1857.

If the job with the park had signaled a new beginning in

Fred's life, this news signaled an end that he could hardly accept. Since his earliest days, John had been somewhere in his life, if not with him, then close in spirit. Now John was gone.

PARK DESIGNER
1857-1858

He almost turned down the next opportunity. Numb with grief, he went each day to the park, eager to work as hard as he could. His one ambition was to wear himself out and go back to his room at night so tired that he could fall asleep at once.

And then Calvert Vaux came to see him. Fred had kept up his acquaintance with this talented, friendly young man ever since meeting him as Andrew Jackson Downing's protégé in Newburgh. In fact, after Downing's death, when Vaux decided to move to New York, he had considered for a while the purchase of Fred's Staten Island farm. However, he had finally decided to live in Manhattan and establish his practice as an architect there.

Now Vaux wanted to talk to Fred about the competition. Fred knew about it, of course. The park commissioners had not been satisfied with the design that Egbert Viele had submitted. They had announced a competition for the best design for Central Park. They were offering $2,000 as a first prize with lesser awards for runners-up. Since the park had been one of Downing's pet projects, Vaux had been interested in it from the beginning. Now he had decided to enter the competition. And he wanted Olmsted to collaborate with him on the design.

"You are daily on the grounds and will have a much clearer picture of the terrain and what is possible to do with it than Viele's map provides," said Vaux.

Fred looked at Vaux for a moment and then said that he did not know if it would be proper for him to collaborate with Vaux. After all, he was employed by Viele who had already submitted his design. Viele might feel that Fred was being insubordinate if he worked on a competitive design.

Vaux suggested that Fred discuss the matter with Viele. He hoped very much that Fred would join him.

The next day, Fred did speak to Viele. The chief engineer looked at Fred with the same coldness that he had shown when Fred first appeared. "Why should it bother me?" he said. "Do what you want to do. I have already worked out the best possible plan for the park, and sooner or later the board will admit it. Do what you want."

Fred nodded and left. But Viele's contempt had roused something in him. Suddenly, he realized that he *wanted* to join Vaux in working out a design for the park. The desire to do so grew in a sort of rush.

He stopped on a rise of land to look out over the acres that had been acquired for a park. He looked east and west and south and north. He thought about the land, and what it might become. He thought about the people in the city—the poor, crowded into their cramped rooms, the toughs, roaming the streets, the hard-working people who managed to scrape out a living but little else. He even thought of the rich, and what they all might need from this land. And he thought about the future—what the city might be in ten, twenty, forty years hence.

Suddenly, it was as though all the things that had concerned him through the years had converged in this one project.

He hurried to Vaux's offices to tell Vaux that he was at his service.

They were different types, Olmsted and Vaux. Olmsted was intense and impetuous—a "truant personality," in his father's words. Vaux was calm, charming, slow to take offense. Olmsted was thinking now of what a park could mean to *people*—how in offering them a place to relax and contemplate nature, they might become happier and able to live together more peacefully and productively. Vaux thought of the park as a work of art—and Fred himself had once written of the "artist who sketches the outline for nature to fill in." But in the last years, his thoughts had turned more to public service.

Actually, as soon as they set to work the differences between them did not matter. Better than that, they complemented each other and the two men understood each other so well that a word or two from one was enough to make the other nod in agreement. And it was fortunate that they did have this understanding, for there was much to do and time was short. It was now late December and the contest ended on the first of April, 1858. Both Calvert and Fred were busy every day with their regular work, which meant they had to cram all their work on the design for the park into the late afternoons and evenings.

Certain requirements had been laid down by the commissioners. Every design had to provide for at least four east-to-west crossings of the park between its southern boundary at

59th Street and its northern boundary at 106th. Also required were provisions for a parade ground, playgrounds, a site for a concert hall, an ornamental fountain, a flower garden, and a place that could be flooded in the winter for skating.

Fred and Calvert considered all the requirements as they pored over the topographic maps of the park's acreage. They talked, they made quick sketches, and then they went out into the busy New York night and took a hansom cab to the park. Night was much the best time to visit. There were no job-hunters beseiging Fred for employment. The acres were dark and quiet. They could move about as they wished.

One thing both were agreed on. They would think of everything in terms of the future. Fred had seen the growth of New York City since his first visits there as a boy. From a little town at the tip of the island it had spread northward, mile after mile. He was sure it would continue to grow and Calvert agreed. Both of them squinted their eyes and envisioned the houses, the churches, the office buildings that would one day spring up on the barren acres on either side of the park site. They even dared think that New York might have a population of 2,000,000 some day.

And so they tackled the problem of the transverse road-ways. One day, they imagined, those roadways would have to carry a great deal of traffic. Livestock from the west side might have to be driven across to the east side or vice versa. Fire engines would have to go racing across. Public traffic of all kinds would need to go back and forth. What would this sort of east-west traffic mean to the quiet walks, drives, and bridle paths they were planning for the park? Must those quiet ways be continually disrupted?

They were never sure which one of them thought of the solution. But suddenly they had it. The transverse crossings should be *sunken* below the level of the park, with bridges over them at appropriate intervals, so that business traffic across the park need never intersect with the strollers, horseback riders, or carriage drivers in the park itself.

It was an inspired solution—a solution that continues to keep the park free from cross-town tangles 130 years later.

So they solved that problem and went on to others, looking at the land and considering what would be most appropriate. For the southern end of the park acreage, which was mostly flat, they contrived the meadows, the malls, the rambles which most suited that area. There too, they arranged that by draining and excavating, a lake could be set aside for freezing in winter, to provide an ice-skating pond. To the north, where the land was rougher, they arranged for more dramatic natural effects.

And all the time Fred was thinking of the people who would be coming to the park. How should they arrange the paths for entrance? How should the arrangements and the plantings give visitors at once a sense that they were in a special place—an outdoor living room?

At last it was time to gather up their sketches and notes and put them together in one master plan which would show the overall design, and then to make a series of small sketches showing in detail how different areas of the park would be improved.

Fred and Calvert worked almost without sleep. They made the basic drawings in meticulous detail, the great sheets spilling over from the drawing tables to the floor. Friends who stopped by were given pens and ink to do their small part by inking in grass or leaves in small drawings that showed profiles of the land as it was and as it might be. The hours went by. The nights went by. Fred's fingers were cramped and ink-stained. So were Calvert's. All their thoughts were concentrated on getting the drawings done in time.

A few months earlier, Fred had been almost sick with grief. Now, though he still felt the loss of his brother, he was happy with his work in a way he had never been before. Later he wrote, "If a fairy had shaped it for me, it could not have fitted me better. It was normal, ordinary and naturally outgrowing from my previous life . . . and it occupied my whole heart."

They finished their drawings just in time for the deadline. On April 1, 1858, the last day of the competition, they delivered their plans for a park that they named "Greensward" to the commissioners. Their entry was one of thirty-five and was numbered 33.

They both had a feeling of letdown. For three months they had thought of nothing but the plan. Now it was gone from them, to compete with thirty-four other designs. They wondered about those other designs. They wondered about the judges. But there was nothing they could do except go back to their usual occupations and wait.

On April 28, two days after Fred's thirty-sixth birthday, the judges announced their decision. By a vote of seven to four, the commissioners had elected to give first prize to entry 33.

Fred and Calvert's "Greensward" had been chosen as the design for New York's park. The two men were named jointly to oversee the working out of this plan for the first real park in the United States.

FAMILY MAN
1858-1859

"Don't let Mary suffer," John had written his brother before he died.

And ever since John's death, Fred had been writing to Mary in Geneva, urging her to return to America with her three children, so that he and all the family in Hartford would be near to help and cheer them in any way possible. In May, 1858, just after Fred and Calvert's success, she arrived.

Fred was at the dock to meet her and small Charley, Charlotte, and the baby Owen, who had been born abroad. It was good to see Mary again, somewhat subdued, but still firm and courageous in spite of her sorrow. Fred had already arranged that she and the children should go to the farm on Staten Island. The farm had been rented for the past year but was now vacant, and it seemed like a logical place for them. Fred took the little family across the harbor and saw them settled in at the farm. Then he went back to Manhattan to begin turning into a reality the park that he and Calvert Vaux had envisioned.

Problems came up right away. They had won the competition, but that did not stop various important people from protesting that they had better ideas than Olmsted's and Vaux's. Two commissioners studied the plan of gracefully curving drives and paths, carefully arranged dells, meadows and vistas, and decided that it would be more appealing if two straight rows of trees were planted to divide the park, east and west. They also thought the sunken roadways were ridiculous. The city would never grow so far uptown that such cross-park roads would be needed. Calvert and Fred were horrified when they heard that these criticisms and suggestions were to be debated by the commissioners. They fretted over what they could do and how they could protect their design. Finally, to their relief, they heard that the Board of Commissioners had voted down any changes in the plan. Olmsted and Vaux were to proceed with their design as it had been submitted.

Work now began to move at a faster rate. Fred, already on the grounds as superintendent, had been appointed architect-in-chief, displacing the disagreeable Viele. Viele was not happy about this and started what commotion he could. But the work went on anyway.

Fred hired an engineer to supervise the drainage and the laying of pipes to bring water to supply a lake. Now Fred was grateful for everything he had learned about drainage on his farms, during his tour of England, even back in the days when he had studied civil engineering. It all helped him to hire the right man and to sensibly oversee his activities. Road builders were hired to construct the carriage drives. Nurserymen were visited to select trees mature enough to give a good effect but still young enough to withstand transplanting. All sorts of suppliers, of bricks, gravel, dynamite, pipes, topsoil, grass, and a hundred other items, had to be consulted. Fred was everywhere, planning, organizing, seeing work to completion.

Meantime, Calvert, who did not enjoy organizing as much as Fred did, was busy with his own special contributions. He was designing the graceful bridges that would take carriage drives over bridle paths below. He was designing the more imposing overpasses that would take park roads over the sunken transverse crossings. He was also designing fountains, shelters, summerhouses, and all sorts of architectural attractions.

By June, Fred was supervising 2,000 workmen in the park. By July, the force had risen to 2,500. But whenever he was able to take a little time, he went to Staten Island to check on the welfare of Mary and the children. He talked with her about the problems he was having and the progress he was making and was cheered by her interest and enthusiasm.

Actually, a great many New Yorkers were beginning to be excited by the progress that was being made. Families came on Sundays to the southern end of the park site and strolled about inspecting the work and the plantings. Other people came in carriages to ride past the grounds and inspect them. In August, when it seemed that a successful cable had been laid underwater across the Atlantic, city officials scheduled a big parade to celebrate this latest modern wonder. Among the marchers was a group of one thousand Central Park workmen, pushing carts and carrying shovels as symbols of their activities. Fred led the contingent, and New Yorkers, gathered along the line of march, cheered the park workers as they went by.

With the first days of fall, Fred grew impatient, eager to get more and more done before the cold weather came and most work would be impossible. Tense as he was, he took time for another trip to Staten Island. This time, he wanted to convince Mary that she and the children should leave the farm and move to the city. He said they would be too uncomfortable on the farm through the long winter. He would not be able to visit so regularly either. Besides, he was able to tell Mary of a brownstone house that was for rent on 79th Street in Manhattan. She would find life much more convenient if she were to move there, he said. Also, he could stop in after his work at the park quite frequently to make sure all was well. Mary did not hesitate for long. Soon she was nodding, saying that if the rent were not too high, she would make the move and would like it very much.

In October, 1858, Mary and the children came to the city and moved into the brownstone house. It was a happy move for everyone. Now Mary could walk up 79th Street to the park and see for herself the progress about which Fred had told her. The trees that had been planted, the shaping of the land, the lake, ready to be a skating rink after the first hard freeze, the wall, running seven miles around the park—there they all were. Now when Fred stopped by of an evening on his way to his own rooms, Mary could listen with understanding to his problems and plans. They had always talked well together. Now they began to share each other's interests as they had never done before. Fred became more than a visiting uncle to the children. He was very like the father they had lost. They ran to him when he came to the house, clambered over him, and asked for stories. Fred was happy to oblige. And his impatience was calmed somewhat by Mary's brisk common sense. Matter-of-factly, she said that of course he had to lay off most of his workers now, and of course there was little he could do until spring. But he could still plan. It was a good winter for Fred and Mary and her family too.

In the spring, Fred began to hire workers again. He was

eager to begin laying sod for the lawns, to do more transplanting and to get to work on the drives and paths. He pressed himself harder and harder, and then, suddenly he was ill. It seemed to be a return of the typhoid fever he had first suffered years before during his time at sea.

Mary worried about him and came to his room to nurse him and see that he was comfortable and fed, until finally he was on his feet again. Somehow, though, by this time, he and Mary realized that they were happier together than apart. And so, in June, 1859, he and Mary were married.

Since his teens, Fred had been fancying himself in love with some girl or another, but never quite enough in love to get married. Now he had found the woman he could love without hesitation. So he became a married man, with a ready-made family as well. He moved in with Mary and the children in the house on 79th Street, and continued to work furiously on the park.

EMBATTLED
1859-1861

He had work that he loved, and at last a wife he loved and who loved him in return. He should have been perfectly happy. Indeed, he might have been, except for the political obstacles that faced him at every turn.

He was almost used to the clamoring jobseekers. These he could survey, hiring some and dismissing the others in spite of their threats and shouts. A worse problem had arisen—the problem of money to pay for the work on the park. One of the members of the Board of Commissioners, a certain Andrew Green, had become director of finances for the park. And though Green was devoted to the idea of the park, he was even more devoted to the idea of not spending an unnecessary penny, and was forever delaying approval of Olmsted's orders for one item or another.

Olmsted grew more and more impatient as he tried to reason with Green and to prove to him that not buying a few more wheelbarrows would mean that sod already purchased could not be planted, which would mean the loss of the sod at a greater expense than the purchase of the wheelbarrows. Green would simply look at Fred, tighten his lips, and shake his head.

Bottling up his frustration, Fred would go home to Mary and the children, too upset to eat or sleep. And of course, after this had gone on long enough, he became ill again. When he could not seem to shake off his exhaustion, Mr. Green suddenly became generous and suggested that Olmsted take a few weeks to study the parks in England and France. He had the board vote five hundred dollars for Olmsted's expenses. Worn out and miserable, Fred talked it over with Mary, who urged him to go. And so at the end of September he was on his way.

The weeks abroad were good for him. He was known now in London and Paris and had a fine time talking to park officials in those cities and visiting public gardens. He felt quite restored when he returned home. While he was away Mary had moved the family, as he had arranged before he left, into an unused convent in the northern section of the park grounds. Fred was delighted to find that everything was comfortable and convenient in the new surroundings. Settling in, he was hopeful that things would go more smoothly in the future.

But any large work undertaken by public financing has a hundred, a thousand, different critics, anxious to question the way their tax money is being used. Fred heard from many of these critics, and always there was Andrew Green, refusing to spend the money to caulk a new bridge, refusing this, refusing that, and checking every bill over and over again.

Fred tried to keep his temper and during the winter worked hard on the next year's budget for the park, trying to allow for all the items he knew would be needed and still keep the figure at a total that Green would approve. It was a relief when Green approved his figures, and Fred went eagerly to work in the spring.

He had a very personal reason for happiness in June when Mary gave birth to a baby boy. Delighted by this, and not displeased by the progress in the park, Fred was ready to continue being as patient as possible in the face of criticism and delays.

And then came the carriage accident. He had taken Mary and the baby out with him in the buggy to try a new horse. They had driven far up into the northern part of Manhattan Island when the horse, tormented by flies, switched his tail and then caught the reins under his tail. Frightened, the animal bolted. Fred stood up to get a better hold on the reins. The carriage lurched against something—a post—a stump— and Fred was flung out of the buggy onto a rock. Mary, still clutching the baby, was tipped out a little farther along. Miraculously, neither she nor the baby was hurt. The baby in her arms, she rushed back to Fred. He was lying, half-conscious, a shattered bone protruding from his trouser leg.

Mary ran to the nearest farmhouse, fortunately not far away. The owners were instantly helpful. The woman of the house took the baby from Mary and a man was dispatched to carry Fred from where he was into the house. They gave him what first aid they could while a doctor was on his way.

When the doctor came he looked grave. Fred's leg had been broken in three places. He murmured something about amputation and then looked again at Fred, thin and pale from all his efforts on the park, and decided the risk would be too great. He set the bones after a fashion and then advised that the poor man be taken home.

For a few days Mary was not sure that Fred would survive.

And then, even as she watched over him, the infant boy who had been unharmed by the carriage accident, suddenly fell ill of the sickness that was the terror of all mothers in the summertime—infant cholera. Within a few days, the baby was dead.

The blow was terrible. Perhaps because he felt he must comfort Mary, Fred began to mend. As the sorrowful days went by, Fred grew stronger. Soon it was plain that one of his legs would always be shorter than the other and that he would walk with a limp, but he was definitely going to live.

Within two months, Mary was driving him in the buggy, his leg propped up on the dashboard, to oversee the work in the park. Being Fred, he was distressed by every evidence of improper work and made dozens of notes.

But that distress was nothing to the blow that came a few weeks later. Mr. Green called him and asked him to explain how it was that he had greatly overspent the money allowed him for the year and to announce that because of this overspending there would be no money at all available for further work on the park during the next year.

Fred was dazed, shocked, and above all, humiliated. For, according to Mr. Green's figures, he had indeed spent much more than he had estimated he would. It really was not his fault. He never had enough helpers in his office to keep any proper accounting of expenses. But it seemed useless, and demeaning as well, to say this to Mr. Green, who was looking at him with pleased satisfaction. What could he say? What could he do?

At home, relating the whole grim story to Mary, and remembering all the obstacles Green had put in his path in the past, Fred finally told her that he thought he had no choice but to resign his post as architect-in-chief. Mary begged him to talk it over with Calvert Vaux.

Vaux, always more patient and tolerant than Olmsted, begged him not to take the matter so personally, to meet with the board and explain the circumstances, and above all not to resign. After all, in spite of the difficulties, the plan which they had evolved together was coming to completion, but it never would be finished properly if Fred resigned.

But the long struggle with Green and with all his other critics had been too much for Fred. He sighed but could not agree with Vaux's counsel. Soon he was writing his letter of resignation and sending it to the Board of Commissioners.

In the feeling of emptiness that followed, he told himself that the completion of a park was a small thing to be concerned about when there was a much greater problem facing the nation—a problem that he had devoted thoughts and efforts to for months and years but which he had almost ignored in the last months.

Slavery! By now, in late 1860, it was no longer a matter of Northern anti-slavery people denouncing the system and Southerners defending it. The two sections of the country were actually splitting apart. The Democratic party had separated into two branches, a northern one and a southern one, and each had nominated a candidate for President. This meant that it was almost certain that the Republican candidate would win in the election that fall.

Fred knew very little about the man whom the Republicans had nominated, Abraham Lincoln of Illinois, except that he was against the spread of slavery. He also knew that several Southern states had already threatened to secede from the Union when and if Lincoln was elected.

Would they really do so? And if they did, then what? Would the North accept their decision? Would two sections of the country split apart into two republics peacefully—or would they go to battle over the issue?

Fred thought they would fight, and that it would be well for people to begin preparing themselves for war. He knew he was unfit to be a soldier himself, half-crippled as he was. But perhaps he could do *something*. Perhaps he could take the three books he had written about the slave states, condense them into one book for easier reading, and have that published. Perhaps such a book might help a bit in strengthening public opinion against slavery and making people more ready to fight against its spread.

He had barely begun to work on that project when word came that the Board of Commissioners for Central Park had considered his resignation, studied the situation, and refused to allow him to resign. He was still architect-in-chief of the park.

Meantime, Lincoln had been elected President. Rumors and alarms flashed around the country, and some of the rumors turned out to be only too true. South Carolina seceded from the Union, followed rapidly by six other Southern states. Southerners in the nation's capital began secretly shipping arms from federal arsenals to the South. There were rumors that Lincoln would be assassinated before he was inaugurated. Fortunately, this alarm proved untrue. He took the oath of office on the steps of the Capitol and pleaded for the cause of the Union, hoping that war could be averted.

But in April, 1861, Southern guns fired on Fort Sumter off Charleston, South Carolina, and the war had begun.

THE SANITARY
COMMISSION
1861-1863

By midsummer of 1861, eager recruits for the Union Army were swarming into Washington, D.C., by the thousands, coming in railway cars, in wagons, on horseback, and on foot. But once arrived, they found no barracks, no commissaries, no provisions for them at all. The Medical Bureau of the army was totally unprepared to deal with men in such numbers and had no idea of how to proceed. And so the men set up rough camps for themselves which soon became pestilential shambles. They slept in mud and dirt. They had little food, most of it spoiled and poorly cooked. They had no sanitary facilities, no provisions for washing or latrines. Inevitably, many men became ill. In the disorder, the stench and the filth, with no one to care for them, many died before they had made even their first try at fighting for the Union.

Horrified by the situation, various civilians banded together and formed what they called the Sanitary Commission —since some sort of sanitation was obviously the first need. With President Lincoln's approval, the Commission went into action, and one of the first things it did was write to Frederick Law Olmsted in New York and ask him to be its executive secretary.

Executive Secretary to a Sanitary Commission? It sounded like an odd post for a man who had found his life's work in designing a beautiful park. But as soon as Olmsted received the letter he realized that this was the war work which he had been seeking. He took a leave of absence from his restored post as architect of the park, told Calvert Vaux to carry on, said good-bye to Mary and the children, and took the train to Washington.

And so began the two-year period of Olmsted's active engagement in the war. They were years during which he traveled to many battlefields, met and grew to know most of the Union generals, and met and came to love Abraham Lincoln. In those years he shaped and organized the Sanitary Commission into a useful national organization for relief and assistance—an organization that would ultimately become the American branch of the Red Cross.

Executive Secretary to the Sanitary Commission—perhaps it was not such a curious post after all, for a man who had long since learned to think in terms of three elements—the land—the people—the future—and then plan ways for them to harmonize.

Certainly he saw enough of misused and poorly chosen land when he toured the mud and filth of the camps around Washington. He saw people, needing proper shelter, proper food and cooking facilities, proper sanitation facilities. And looking into the future, he could see how those needs would multiply a hundredfold when real battles began. After tramping about all day, he went back to his hotel room to write up his findings on the campsites, the food, the clothing, the diseases and the nursing and hospital facilities. Then he made his own recommendations about how the Medical Bureau, the army, the government, or the Sanitation Commission should act to meet these basic problems.

But making recommendations was a simpler thing than getting any action taken on them. Career army officers, jealous of rank and privilege, fought the idea of any changes in the system. Congressmen, protecting votes at home, had other objections. Various committed individuals, like Dorothea Dix, Superintendent of Nurses, were also jealous of their own provinces. Olmsted wondered if he had any hope of changing anything.

But he kept at it. Day after day and long into every night, he worked for a reformation of the Medical Bureau of the army and did some politicking himself, to try to get a new Surgeon General appointed. He followed the battle news, and when various groups of slaves in the South were freed by Northern troops, he offered a plan for hiring them as free laborers to work the cotton fields where they had formerly worked as slaves. It was the sort of plan for preparing former slaves for freedom that had long been dear to him.

During the Peninsular Campaign in Virginia, he set up a hospital ship transport service to bring wounded soldiers back from Virginia to Washington, D.C., for treatment. It was rugged work, with Olmsted in the middle of it all, just as he had been with the park. One old ocean liner, the *Daniel Webster*, which was anchored in the Potomac, was cleaned up and fitted with hospital supplies. Then, accompanied by a group of volunteer nurses and doctors and a crew of sailors, Olmsted sailed with the ship down the coast to the mouth of the York River, near which many Union troops were camped.

As soon as the *Webster* was loaded with ill and wounded soldiers and on its way back to Washington, Olmsted went to work to make ready another ship that had been turned over to the Commission.

A battle farther inland had just ended, and the need for hospital facilities was so great that disabled men were crawling aboard this second transport, the *Ocean Queen*, before any proper arrangements had been made. Women volunteers tried to improvise hot food for the suffering men out of Indian meal and water. Olmsted himself was everywhere, dividing the ship into wards, some for the very sick, some for those with infectious diseases, some for those who were simply exhausted. Somehow, he acquired bedding, food supplies, more volunteer doctors and nurses, and planned schedules for them, so that all tasks would be done and someone would always be in attendance on the sick. And all the while, more patients were being brought to the ship—by tugboat, by wagon, or half-carried by their comrades.

One way or another, Olmsted and the tireless men and women helping him accomplished the miracle. Every man had a good place to sleep, a hot meal, and was given medical attention. Finally, the ship, loaded with eleven hundred men, sailed off to Washington.

After this, the hospital transport service operated regularly until the end of that campaign in Virginia, rescuing hundreds of wounded men from almost certain death. The service not only saved these men but made the work of the Sanitary Commission better known to the public, which meant, in turn, that it was easier to raise funds for its work.

That service established, Olmsted worked to get more and better hospital tents in Washington, D.C. Equipment there was so scarce that some wounded men were simply laid out on blankets on the White House lawn.

After that, he took off on a long journey through the Midwest, visiting the Sanitary Commissions that had been set up in those areas and trying to coordinate their work with the work in the East.

On this journey, Olmsted met a stocky, cigar-smoking general whom he liked at once, a modest but determined man named Ulysses Grant, whom he thought might be the best man the Union Army had. After that, he traveled east again and arrived in time for the battle at Gettysburg where the tide finally turned in favor of the North.

He had little time to rejoice over the victory, but was on his feet for hours every day, touring the makeshift hospitals that had been set up for the Gettysburg wounded. He did what he could to organize the confusion, arranging for the transport of the wounded who could be moved, ordering and arranging for the delivery of more supplies.

Soon came the news of the Union success at Vicksburg, Mississippi, where General Grant more than justified Olmsted's impression of him as a soldier who knew what he was doing.

Not long after that, with the fortunes of the North on the upswing at last, Olmsted resigned his post with the Sanitary Commission.

He had a variety of reasons for doing so. Perhaps most importantly, he felt that he had done as much as he could in organizing the Commission and that someone else could now take over. He was also weary of the political battles that went along with every attempt to make a change. Along with that, he was exhausted and half-sick from the long hours and constant efforts that he had demanded of himself to do the job properly.

And, of course, there was the fact that he was still Frederick Olmsted, who was always inclined to shift from one activity, once he had solved its problems, to another that offered new challenges—Frederick, who had a "truant disposition."

THE FAR WEST
1863-1865

So now, as the war raged on in the East and the Midwest, Olmsted spent more than two years in the Far West, in the wild and rugged interior of northern California. His job— superintendent of a vast property, the Mariposa Estates, which contained a dozen or more working gold mines.

He was not forgetting the war, but felt his usefulness was over. As for Central Park, that seemed like a dream to him to which he could never return. Politicians had taken over the construction of the park and its management to such a degree that Calvert Vaux had finally resigned, both for himself and for Olmsted in May of 1863. Olmsted did not even want to think about the park. And certainly the Far West was as different from those eastern acres as any land could be.

Olmsted was not sure just how he felt about western scenery as he rode his horse northward and eastward from San Francisco toward the mining property. He saw a dry, brown, barren landscape rimmed with jagged mountains. "I really don't understand it & won't say whether it is beautiful or not," he wrote home to Mary. But that was during the dry season of the early fall and he had not yet come to the foot-hills of the Sierra Nevada Mountains where the Mariposa mines were located.

After he started traveling through the properties to inspect the various mines and learn about their operations, he began to appreciate the special character of this western land and to admire it. And when at last he was able to journey up through the mountains to Yosemite Valley, he saw landscapes that daz-zled and awed him. They were entirely different from scenes to which he was accustomed in the East and the South—so overpowering that they remained forever somewhat strange to him. But he did know them at once for what they were— wonders of nature with which man should never tamper. Many areas of the earth were and could be actually improved by man's attentions and activities. Here, with the awesome peaks surrounding the fantastic valley, nature seemed no longer to be humanity's partner, but a great god to be wor-shipped.

Feeling that way about the Yosemite area, Fred was very pleased when news came from the East that President Lin-coln, in the midst of his wartime cares and anxieties, had taken time to sign a bill that removed the Yosemite Valley from the government lands open to settlement, and ceded it to the state of California to be held sacred forever for public resort and recreation.

He was surprised, but also pleased, to learn that he had been appointed one of the commissioners to administer the valley as a public park. Soon he was arranging for the area to be surveyed and mapped, and was beginning to write a long report on his recommendations as to how the park should be approached by various roads that would not encroach on the wilderness, how building, except for a few shelters, should be prohibited, and so on.

These were satisfactions, real and solid. There were other satisfactions. After he was settled in a house on the mining property, Mary and the family came from the East to join him. Before long, the whole family was taking camping trips together in the mountains—even the baby, Marion, born soon after the war began, came along, carried on horseback by her mother or father.

But the mining venture itself, which had seemed so promising to the New York bankers who had hired Olmsted to oversee it, gradually began to prove less and less profitable. Olmsted worked hard, organizing the operations for more efficiency, planning ways to make life on the Mariposa property less primitive. He envisioned how fertile the Mariposa valley could become with proper irrigation and worked out a scheme for a canal. But it was not his fault that the mines put into operation in the first enthusiasm of the gold rush were at the wrong end of the Mariposa properties, nor had he any way of knowing where more productive ventures could be started.

Still, as the mines produced less and less gold, the banker-owners in the East began to lose interest in that property and to show signs of giving up on the whole venture.

Olmsted was disappointed. He had dreamed some splendid dreams for the land that the Mariposa Mining Company owned, dreams that would have made the land richer and more satisfying in the future.

But he had acquired other interests also in the West by this time. He spent a good deal of time in the mushrooming city of San Francisco, where he was known not only for his connection with the mining company but as a landscape designer, one of the creators of New York's Central Park. As a result he was asked to lay out plans for a new College of California, to be located across the bay from San Francisco. He was asked to design a cemetery in Oakland and to plan the landscapes for the homes of several rich men who lived near San Francisco. Working on these projects, he wondered if his own future lay in the West, whatever happened to the Mariposa Mining Company.

But from the beginning, he was never out of touch with the East and what was happening there. He rejoiced with every news report of Union victories, and despaired at Union defeats. He followed the fortunes of the Sanitary Commission and felt great satisfaction when it seemed that its work was proceeding well.

Calvert Vaux wrote to him frequently. One letter carried the news that Vaux had been asked to plan and create a park like Central Park for New York's sister city across the East River, Brooklyn, but Vaux did not want to take on the project unless Olmsted would collaborate with him as before. Soon Vaux was writing that the commissioners of Central Park were seriously considering reinstating both himself and Olmsted to their original posts as architects of the park. "Come back and join me," Vaux wrote again and again.

Olmsted thought a good deal about Vaux's entreaties. In many ways, he was tempted. He missed the East. He had loved Central Park from the beginning. He would like to finish it as it should be finished, and he was sure he would enjoy creating another park of a similar nature in Brooklyn. Still, he hesitated.

Wonderful news came to the West in April of 1865. Grant had finally battered Lee and the Confederates into surrender. The Union had been preserved. Slavery had been abolished. But before Fred or anyone else had really savored the sense of thanksgiving, there came the tragic news that Lincoln had been assassinated. Mary draped the doorway of the house in Mariposa valley with black crape and she and Olmsted both tried to make the children understand that a very great man had died.

Through the summer, Olmsted worked at finishing up his duties at the Mariposa mines. He also went to San Francisco to study the grounds and draw up plans for the college which would later be known as Berkeley.

With a group of important politicians and businessmen, he made another trip to Yosemite. As they gathered under the great trees, the peaks looming around them, he read his proposals on how this magnificent valley should be managed as a national park. He had his plans for the access roads and various shelters. He had figures on how much it would cost to make these improvements, which would make the area more accessible to the public but still leave it unspoiled.

In this report, he also recommended that steps be taken to create more national parks across the nation. Many areas of great natural beauty and wonder should be set aside so that they would not be spoiled by commerce but saved for the enjoyment of the people for all time.

The men who were listening nodded as he finished and congratulated him later on the report, but nothing was done about his proposals and recommendations for some time. Still, Olmsted's proposals were those that were ultimately followed to create Yosemite National Park, and his suggestion for a number of parks across the country planted the seed that would one day flower in a great network of national parks.

He did not have much success with another project either. This was a park for the city of San Francisco. Olmsted studied the land that had been suggested and pondered its nature. He thought about the possible dangers of earthquakes, and also of fires in that periodically dry area, and how a park might help guard against them. He made hundreds of notes and many sketches, full of imaginative solutions to the special problems that were presented by San Francisco's location, soil, and climate. Ultimately, he drew up one quite remarkable plan, which might have done much to halt the spread of San Francisco's disastrous fire forty years later—but that plan was never adopted by the city.

However, his final drawing for this plan was still not completed when Olmsted decided that he had been long enough in the West.

The Board of Commissioners of Central Park had indeed reappointed him and Vaux to resume their original posts. Vaux was insisting also that Olmsted join him in planning Brooklyn's park. The work Olmsted loved the best was beckoning. Along with all this, a friend from his publishing days, Edwin Godkin, had finally acquired the backing to publish a new magazine, the *Nation*, which would champion many of the causes in which Olmsted was interested, and Godkin wanted Olmsted to join him as co-founder and editor.

In the fall of 1865, Olmsted and his family packed up and embarked on the long sea voyage down the coast and around South America to return to the East and New York.

LANDSCAPE ARCHITECT
1865-1893

And so he came back to the work that he had discovered as his own just eight years before. And having come back, after so many detours, he would continue with it for the next thirty years, the rest of his working life.

He would still make detours and involve himself briefly with other activities now and then. Soon after his return to New York he spent a great deal of time helping to edit the new magazine, the *Nation*. Some years later, he was much involved in founding the Metropolitan Museum of Art in New York, and though he had fought against any buildings being erected in Central Park, in the end he was not dissatisfied when the great classical structure to house the museum was located on the edge of the park on Fifth Avenue.

He also struggled through more political difficulties during the years when he and Vaux were finishing Central Park and working on Prospect Park in Brooklyn. Both he and Vaux

fought against the use of parks as great "pork-barrels," especially after "Boss" Tweed and his Tammany organization
took control of New York's government. Mostly, they fought
in vain. Many of their overall plans were changed or ignored.
To make jobs for cronies, gangs of men were hired to grub
out some of Olmsted's most special plantings. There came a
time when Olmsted could not look at Central Park without a
feeling of despair. At one point he resigned once again as an
architect, was rehired as a consultant, and then finally dis-
missed.

But all of these difficulties and detours were not really so
important after all. Because, during those thirty years, first
with Vaux, and then with other partners, Olmsted was engaged in planning and designing—not just parks, but villages,
colleges, estates, towns, factories, capitols, resorts—almost
every sort of place, large or small, in which people lived,
worked or played. Every place that involved land—people—
and the future.

Olmsted and Vaux worried for a time over what to call
themselves when they went into business together after Olmsted's return. What they did was really something new. Not
many people understood their work as a real profession.
Should they call themselves "landscape designers," "landscape artists," "landscape gardeners," or "landscape architects"? They ruled out "gardeners" at once, for that gave the
impression of men who simply decorated a landscape. They
rejected "artists," for even though they worked as artists,
their concern was also very much with what was practical,
what was convenient and appropriate. Finally, without being
altogether satisfied, they decided to call their new firm Olmsted, Vaux and Company, Landscape Architects.

So as Landscape Architects, they went forth to design the
Brooklyn park, which Olmsted finally considered more satis-

factory than Central Park. Together and singly, they took on a variety of other assignments, for as the country grew, a certain number of people were beginning to recognize that planning for the future could be more satisfactory than letting everything happen haphazardly.

Two new agricultural colleges, one being established in Massachusetts and one in Maine, asked Olmsted to draw up plans for them. As always, he considered the nature of the land, the aims of the institution (in this case, to train young men to be good farmers), and how those aims could best be met. For both colleges, he suggested a group of pleasant homelike structures, where the best aspects of living on and with the land could be practiced along with learning in classes. In both cases, the committees to approve the final designs decided they preferred some grand tall building set up in the middle of a vacant field.

Olmsted refused to be discouraged. He was determined to believe that sooner or later, people would see that what was appropriate and convenient was ultimately the most beautiful and useful.

He and Vaux planned a park system for Boston. Seeing the city bounded by water, with no free space in a central area, they designed a green belt of narrow parks to follow the shoreline around the city.

Olmsted designed a park for Montreal in Canada, on the site of its one looming hill, Mont Royal. He plotted the roads, following the rising contours of the land through picturesque slopes and hollows to the summit with its spreading view.

Because they were very aware of how the growth of cities was causing people who could afford it to move out into the countryside within commuting distance, Olmsted and Vaux were pleased by a commission to design a suburban village for a tract of land west of Chicago. Olmsted spent days on the land, envisioning the ways people would travel to and from the city, the way that plots should be laid out so that each home had a pleasant area around it, access to driveways, delivery wagons, and so on. A charming design was laid out for the suburb of Riverside, and work was well advanced when money difficulties forced the developers to stop. Still, Olmsted's vision had reached many people and left a picture in their minds of what a suburban village could be like.

New York City was still growing, just as Olmsted and Vaux had predicted it would. It was ready for another park, north of Central Park, on a slope so steep that real estate men had washed their hands of it. For this site, Olmsted and Vaux created the dramatic Morningside Park, with steps that wound gradually down the slope, interrupted by pleasant little plazas for resting and admiring the views. Later, Olmsted designed a park and a winding driveway along the Hudson River on the upper west side of Manhattan—Riverside Park and Riverside Drive.

Various events, happy and sad, starred Olmsted's life during these years. In 1870, he and Mary had a son. Olmsted named him Frederick Law Olmsted, Jr., looking forward to the day when this son would carry on his work in the new profession of landscape architecture.

In 1872, Olmsted and Vaux decided to dissolve their partnership and work independently. They had learned much from each other, but now it seemed that Vaux would be happier if he concentrated on building, while Olmsted continued to think chiefly about land and the way people used it.

Olmsted's father died the next year. Eighty-two years old, John Olmsted had lived to see his son with the "truant disposition" who had tried so many careers, create for himself a new sort of career. Fred grieved for the father who had always been so generous and understanding.

The education of his own children concerned him. There were five now—John, Charlotte, and Owen, his brother John's children, and his own two, Marion and young Fred, Jr., called Rick. Olmsted was determined that none of them would be subjected to the harsh and discouraging sort of discipline that he had known when he was studying with the Reverend Brace. He would make sure that all of them had the widest, most liberal sort of education.

Meantime, he was busy with professional assignments that now came in a steady stream. He was asked to advise on the landscaping of the state capitol in Albany, New York, and worked on that project with the architect, Henry Hobson Richardson, a man who endeared himself to Olmsted by understanding at once the need for the designer of a building and the designer of the land around it to work together.

He worked as well on the Capitol grounds in Washington, D.C. Through the years many talented architects had worked on the Capitol buildings, which had gradually evolved into stately and imposing structures, but the grounds around them had been mostly ignored. Olmsted visited Washington several times, remembering not only the years he had worked there during the war, but his early visits there as a child, when the city was a straggling town. He saw that though the city had grown, it still straggled, which did not seem right for the capital of a great nation.

He recommended that all the land around the Capitol, all the way to the White House, be considered a single landscape. The plantings around the various government buildings that lined Pennsylvania Avenue were as whimsical and varied as the architecture of the buildings. Olmsted offered a plan that would coordinate all the landscaping into a harmonious whole, and he suggested as well, a green belt of trees along the base of Capitol Hill, which would give healthful shade in the heat of Washington summers.

In the end, Congress would not approve such a large plan. Olmsted's efforts had to be concentrated on the Capitol and its hill. So he focused there on the need for combining open spaces and many approaches, with shade and vistas on the east side of the building. He planned a marble terrace to surround the north, west, and south sides of the building, to create a more formal approach from the lower part of the hill. Then he arranged for the dredging, draining, replacing of soil and planting of trees to make the approach to this terrace both imposing and elegant.

While the work on the Capitol moved along slowly, he was busy with a project which was simply a labor of love. He wanted to rescue Niagara Falls from the commercial blight that surrounded them. Surely those falls, which he remembered first seeing as a child, were a natural wonder which should be preserved unspoiled for generations to come, just as the Yosemite Valley should be kept unchanged.

This was a project that meant campaigning to make people in general aware of what was being destroyed by the confusion of shops, inns, mills, icehouses, flumes, signboards, and fences that had been built around the falls. Olmsted urged all his influential friends to write letters to the newspapers, to the legislature, to the governor, to write articles for magazines, to get up petitions, and to go on speaking tours to waken people to the need for action. He wrote hundreds of letters himself and did a lot of private speaking.

He felt rewarded for all his efforts when a bill was finally passed to make Niagara Falls a public trust. Later, a man who had worked with him wrote, "Success was obtained by the cooperation of multitudes: but the indispensable factor was Mr. Frederick Law Olmsted's thought. He was the real source as he was the true director of the movement."

In 1881, Olmsted decided to move his family and his offices from New York City to the quieter surroundings of Brookline, Massachusetts, just outside of Boston. By this time, his stepson, John, was old enough to help in the management of the office which was busier than ever. It was a great comfort to Olmsted to have this steady, intelligent young man in charge when he himself had to be away for long periods of time.

He was away a great deal now, traveling all over the country. One of his assignments came from California, where Senator Leland Stanford and his wife wanted to establish a university as a memorial for their young son who had died at the age of sixteen. Off he went to California, to design plans that took account of the special nature of the land around Palo Alto, and to try to convince Mr. Stanford that New England landscapes would be neither appropriate nor beautiful in that environment.

Another year he traveled southward into North Carolina, which he had not visited since his journeying through that state in the days before the Civil War. This time he went at the request of young George Vanderbilt, a great-grandson of the old Commodore who had made a fortune in steamships and railroading during the years when Olmsted himself was growing up.

Young Vanderbilt had bought a two-thousand-acre tract of land outside of Asheville, North Carolina, on which he planned to build a beautiful mansion with properly landscaped grounds and gardens. He also wanted to turn the larger part of the property into a great park in the English style.

Olmsted toured the property with him and suggested that the land was more suitable for a scientifically managed forest. This would be something new in the United States and would profit the country as well as give Vanderbilt an interesting occupation. Vanderbilt agreed, and Olmsted was engaged for several years in overseeing the working out of his plans in connection with the building of the mansion itself which had been designed by the popular architect, Richard Morris Hunt.

For years, it seemed, he was crisscrossing the country, which had grown so much and changed so much in the years since he was a boy, traveling with his father in search of picturesque views.

Finally, there were the journeys to Chicago, where a great world's fair was to be held in 1893, commemorating the discovery of America by Columbus four hundred years previously. The nation's most famous artists, architects, and sculptors had been summoned to design the buildings and their decorations for this Columbian Exposition of '93. Olmsted was summoned to draw up the master plan, to coordinate all the different buildings that were planned so that they would look well together, and to design the general appearance of the fair.

MASTER PLANNER
1893-1903

"White City" they called it, because finally, all the buildings erected to house the exhibits of the fair, whatever the style of their architecture, were painted white. It made for a dazzling city-within-a-city there by the edge of Lake Michigan on the south side of Chicago. It was a brilliant world all its own, the white of its buildings offset by the massed greenery of trees, shrubs, and lawns, with streams and lagoons here and there adding the shimmer and cool look of water.

"White City" was a triumph in 1893, when millions came from all over the country and from overseas as well, to walk its promenades, to go from exhibit to exhibit, and to rest, now and then, under shady trees, with views both gracious and inspiring on every side.

Olmsted's contributions to this success did not go unnoticed. His plans to coordinate the efforts of so many different architects, artists, and exhibitors into a framework that provided convenient, appropriate, and beautiful surroundings for all were recognized at a banquet just before the fair opened. The fair's director toasted him, saying: "Each of you knows the name and the genius of him who stands first in the heart and confidence of American artists . . . He it is who has been our best adviser and common mentor. In the highest sense he is the planner of the Exposition—Frederick Law Olmsted."

But ultimately, it was not the planning of the Exposition that was Olmsted's greatest achievement. After the fair was over, those buildings, so imposing to see but basically so flimsy, were torn down. There remained a beautiful park, created out of what had once been swampland.

There it was, Jackson Park—just as Frederick Olmsted had planned it—rich with the planting native to the region, laced with paths and roadways, studded with lakes and islands, to be a joy to the people of Chicago through all the years to come.

The land—the people—the future. One way or another they had always been Frederick Law Olmsted's concern. And now that he was in his seventies, he was being recognized for the pioneer that he was. Both Yale and Harvard Universities conferred the honorary degree of Doctor of Letters on him— once, long ago, a boy who had dropped out of school at fourteen, now a bent and bearded man who still had intent and piercing eyes.

The land—the people who used it—the needs and possibilities of both in the future continued to concern him. He went on with the work on Vanderbilt's estate in North Carolina. He was busy with designs for Boston's Arboretum. And he took great pleasure in the fact that his son Frederick was indeed following in his footsteps. Young Frederick had worked through two summers, helping to carry out his father's instructions on the fair grounds in Chicago. He had studied according to his father's wishes all the subjects that Olmsted thought would enable him to pursue the new career of landscape architect.

Olmsted was still busy with a variety of projects in 1895 when his memory began to fail him. The doctors thought perhaps he had suffered a stroke. But there seemed little they could do. From being vaguely forgetful, Olmsted suddenly became a very old man, confused and unsure.

Fortunately, Mary was still beside him. Fortunately, John was a sturdy rock, managing the business in Brookline. Fortunately, Frederick was ready by now to take over the planning of the many projects that had been assigned to the firm.

Once, long ago, he had been a truant. Now he wandered off into shadows that were not so happy as those he had known when he was young. Finally, the family decided that he would be safest and most comfortable in a hospital cottage in Waverly, Massachusetts. He had himself designed the landscaping around the hospital. Perhaps it was sad that this landscaping was something that he remembered and it displeased him that his design had not been followed. "They didn't carry out my plan, confound them."

He was right, too—very few of the plans he had made in his life had been followed altogether as he had envisioned them. Still, when he died in 1903, the whole idea of planning was no longer as strange to Americans as it had been when he was born, eighty-one years earlier.

The cities rise up all around—tower on tower, windowed walls look on windowed walls.

But in most of those cities across the nation, there is an

oasis somewhere. A place where green things grow, where people can stroll and see the various comforting shapes of nature.

He helped to show the way.

BIBLIOGRAPHY

Olmsted, Frederick Law. "The Beginning of Central Park; A fragment of Autobiography, (ca. 1877)." Reprinted in *Landscape into Cityscape.*

————. *The Cotton Kingdom; A Traveller's Observations on Cotton and Slavery.* New York and London, 1861.

————. *A Journey in the Seaboard Slave States, with Remarks on Their Economy.* New York, 1856.

————. *A Journey Through Texas; or, a Saddle-Trip on the Southwestern Frontier.* New York: Dix, Edwards and Co., 1857.

————. *The Slave States.* Harvey Wish, ed. New York: G. P. Putnam's, 1959.

————. *The Spoils of the Park, with a Few Leaves from the Deepladen Notebooks of "A Wholly Unpractical Man."* Detroit, 1882.

————. *Walks and Talks of an American Farmer in England.* Ann Arbor: University of Michigan Press, 1967.

Olmsted, Frederick Law, Jr., and Theodora Kimball, eds. *Forty Years of Landscape Architecture: Frederick Law Olmsted, Sr.* New York: G. P. Putnam's, 1922.

Barlow, Elizabeth and Alex, William. *Frederick Law Olmsted's New York.* New York: Praeger, 1972.

Fein, Albert. *Frederick Law Olmsted and the American Environmental Tradition.* New York: Braziller, 1972.

Hubbard, Henry Vincent and Kimball, Theodora. *An Introduction to the Study of Landscape Design.* New York: Macmillan, 1917.

Roper, Laura Wood. *FLO, A Biography of Frederick Law Olmsted.* Baltimore: Johns Hopkins University Press, 1973.

19th Annual Report: American Scenic and Historic Preservation Society, Albany, 1914.

Olmsted Papers, Library of Congress.

Files of the *New York Post,* 1845 and following.

Files of *The New York Times,* 1851 and following.

INDEX

ABOUT THE AUTHOR

JOHANNA JOHNSTON's writing talent ranges from adult biographies to books for the very young. A particular interest in bringing to life great figures of the past and a broad knowledge of American history have led to many of her books, including *Together in America; A Special Bravery; Paul Cuffee, America's First Black Captain; The Indians and the Strangers; Women Themselves.*

For several years Miss Johnston wrote for radio, specializing in programs for children. Among her titles for the picture book age are the Edie stories, the ever-popular *Sugarplum,* and *Who Found America?*

Johanna Johnston was born and educated in Chicago, Illinois, and now lives and works in New York City.